the Colonial Revival House

the Colonial Revival House

RICHARD GUY WILSON

PHOTOGRAPHY BY NOAH SHELDON

Harry N. Abrams, Inc., Publishers

Contents

Endurance
WORLD WAR II TO THE PRESENT · 175

Why Colonial Revival?

The Colonial Revival is the United States's most popular and characteristic expression. Neither a formal style nor a movement, Colonial Revival embodies an attitude that looks to the American past for inspiration and selects forms, motifs, and symbols for replication and reuse. Under the Colonial Revival umbrella are buildings and architecture, furniture and decorative arts, landscape and gardens, novels and literature, illustration and painting, sculpture and music.

For many people, the most classic expression of the Colonial Revival occurs in the single-family house, but it also appears in skyscrapers, churches, city halls, libraries, gas stations, post offices, schools, and indeed almost every building type. Some element of Colonial Revival exists in every American town; it is our national architectural idiom. This book concentrates on the single-family house, using it as a vehicle for understanding the Colonial Revival, though the larger context will intrude at times. The house developed very early in American history and it has evolved into being one of the identifying features of American culture, becoming an element of politics, religion, and reform. In contrast to the architecture of most other cultures, American architecture is in many ways a history of the single-family house and how architects have seen and reformed it.

What do we mean by the term *Colonial Revival house*? What images does it bring to mind? To some people it evokes the typical New England stockade-styled house with a big overhang at the front and, inside, a great cooking hearth around which the family would be clustered. Wallace Nutting (1861–1941), at various times a minister, an important Colonial Revival furniture manufacturer, and a restorer of early homes, felt that the early hearth was "the glowing source from which emanated all humane civilizing currents."[1]

For some, the typical Colonial Revival house is not unlike the fine two-story Georgian-style mansion that American poet Henry Wadsworth Longfellow lived in. For others, it is the large brick-faced, porticoed James River estates in Virginia or George Washington's Mount Vernon (1743–ca. 1780). The great Potomac River porch of Washington's house ranks as one of the most imitated architectural motifs in America, appearing in almost every town across the country.

There are still more images associated with the Colonial Revival house, including the Cape Cod cottage and the Dutch Colonial variation. Independence Hall (1731) in Philadelphia, a form that has inspired the design of many buildings for businesses and institutions, was of course not a house but a "state house" for the colony of Pennsylvania. However, the great steeple atop Independence Hall's tower is itself a Colonial Revival design, having been added in 1828. Farther afield, the term *Colonial Revival* is applied to houses that adopt the style of Spanish missions of the Southwest and California. Another variation is the Spanish Colonial that became very popular in Texas, Florida, and California in the 1920s and 1930s and continues today. Throughout much of the Gulf Coast region and the Mississippi River valley—territory once owned by France—there exist the architectural remains of a French, or Creole, Colonial Revival. The term *Colonial Revival* is broad and includes many styles.

Colonial America was not a monolith but contained many groups, and the term *colonial* has been and continues to be indiscriminately linked with an elastic date range.[2] *Colonial* in American history usually means the period of initial European settlement to the achievement of independence (1607 in Jamestown, Virginia; or 1620 in Plymouth, Massachusetts) to 1783 and the Treaty of Paris. Also considered part of the legacy of the colonial era are Spanish- and French-style buildings that date into the nineteenth century. States such as Texas and California were, in a sense, colonies up to the date of their independence, 1836 and 1846, respectively, or to the origination of their statehoods in 1845 and 1850. The term *Colonial Revival* came to encompass post–Revolutionary War buildings of not just the subsequent decade, but through the so-called Federal period (1780–1820), and also the Greek and Roman revivals that thrived between the 1820s and 1860s. One very popular Colonial Revival idiom of the 1890s through the 1910s was the large columnar house known as the "Southern Colonial," which in many ways recalled the typical antebellum plantation house.

Thomas O. Barlow, after Thomas Pritchard Rossiter and Louis Mignet, *The Home of Washington,* or *Washington and Lafayette at Mount Vernon, 1784,* 1859, engraving.

The complex Colonial Revival image mirrors the many motives behind its utilization. The Colonial Revival has a multivalent character; throughout its history it has had many meanings and there have been many different causes for its employment. Why this multivalent character developed will occupy parts of this book, but some preliminary remarks are appropriate. On one level, certain elements of the Colonial Revival involve honoring and celebrating the past. The invention of the modern nation state—such as the United States—brought with it the necessity of creating a new allegiance, not to royalty, but to country. Central to history is not just memory but also artifacts that help convey meaning and inspiration. The Founding Fathers were well aware of the importance of tangible elements of the past. Thomas Jefferson argued for the preservation of the house where he wrote the Declaration of Independence: "Small things, may, perhaps, like the relics of saints, help to nourish our devotion to this holy bond of our Union."[3]

A fascination with early America led many architects to act as preservationists while at the same time drawing inspiration from this work for their new designs. One of the great American preservation efforts, Colonial Williamsburg, Virginia, is in many ways a Colonial Revival town of the 1930s. Many of the saved or preserved colonial houses are really more Colonial Revival since frequently they have been extensively altered. The issue of what is a colonial house was addressed by a Charles Addams cartoon of 1946, but it could be appropriate for any date in the past hundred years.

Influencing many Colonial Revival projects, especially the American house and popular notions of it, is the image of the woman of the house. An argument can be made that women played a substantial role in the development of historic preservation in this country and also in creating the ideology that lay behind the Colonial Revival.[4]

Other motives for Colonial Revival involve ancestor worship and pride in genealogy. Instrumental on this front have been organizations such as the Pilgrim Society, the Association for the Preservation of Virginia Antiquities, the Society for the Preservation of New England Antiquities, and the

Wallace Nutting, *Slanting Sun Rays*, ca. 1915,
hand-tinted platinum print.

Colonial Dames, who have also aided in preservation efforts
and have erected buildings drawing from colonial-era styles.
Whether intended for domestic use or otherwise, building in
the Colonial Revival idiom enables one to create an image of
the past, even to invent a past.

Americans are often characterized as lacking a past. Today,
more and more, we hear of reports concerning the absence of
historical awareness among the country's youth, or some other
group. Colonial Revival, with its invented sense of tradition, can
serve as an instrument of instruction. Examples include George
Boughton's painting *Puritans Going to Church* (1867), which
assisted in teaching students about Thanksgiving. Painters
such as Edwin Howland Blashfield argued that murals of historical figures served as a "public and municipal educator" for
the "uneducated Irishman, German, Swede, [and] Italian."[5]
How to instruct the so-called foreigner in American values
concerned many individuals in the late nineteenth and early
twentieth centuries. The institutionalization of the teaching
of American history at several grade levels was one method,
but eventually the environment—the architecture—itself
became an instrument of instruction. An article on school

design claimed, "Special emphasis is laid upon the traditions
of the early building along the Atlantic seaboard, because it is
the principles of the Fathers of the Republic which we are
endeavoring to instill into our alien races." Explicitly xenophobic was another writer, who said: "We look to the teaching
in public schools to help in the great problem of Americaniz-
ing our mixed people; why not make the buildings themselves
a part of the teaching of the appreciation of architecture?"[6]

Another aspect of the Colonial Revival is the American
spirit of commerce and consumption. Americans love their
colonial past; its allure sells houses and furniture, and it
sparks tourism. In a sense Colonial Revival is a marketing
tool, and identifying one's house with George Washington or
John Adams ostensibly increases its value and salability. Sears,
Roebuck and Company believed this to be true when they
gave historic names to houses in their catalog of homes.

Colonial Revival also exists on the printed page. Historical
novels along with books and articles written by architects,
preservationists, and historians portrayed the forms and
details of colonial houses. While this romance with the past
does not always fare very well in the hands of certain scholars
and critics, for many people these writings provided a picture
of the colonial past and the houses and environments in
which important events took place.[7]

Colonial Revival, in all of its manifestations, acts as an instructive tool, informing people how to live—what their house and furnishings should look like—while providing models of behavior, community, and religious worship. How we literally view the past—whether as tourists on a back road in New England admiring a clapboard house, or browsing an antiques shop in pursuit of pewter dishes, or walking down Duke of Gloucester Street in Colonial Williamsburg—is part of the Colonial Revival phenomenon. In some cases, its appeal comes down to a quest for simplicity and a yearning for the "good old days," while in others it is about having a protective barrier from modernism and present-day traumas. In all of its modes, however, Colonial Revival acts as part of the national memory and helps uphold our cultural identity.

Colonial Revival has been interpreted as distinctly anti-modern in the sense that it offers a safe harbor from the pressures of modern urban life.[8] Obviously modernization, or modernity, occurred not just in America but also internation-

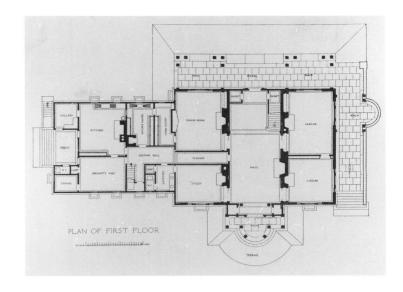

PLAN OF FIRST FLOOR

ally, and similar quests for the comforts of the past took place outside the United States. The Colonial Revival's emphasis on home, hearth, and the image of the family offered a respite from the strain of change, whether in the nineteenth, twentieth, or twenty-first century. That the neurasthenia prevalent during the turn of the twentieth century led to a retreat into the past (a currently popular view) is a dubious

BELOW: McKim, Mead & White, Henry A. C. Taylor House, Newport, Rhode Island, 1883–85. Garden facade.

RIGHT: Taylor House. Plan.

theory, unless depression has gripped most of the Western world for the past two centuries.[9]

Out of this need for a historical identity, Americans have created a pantheon of emblematic individuals, places, and objects—Plymouth Rock, John Hancock, Mount Vernon, the missions of the American West and Southwest, tall case clocks, and *Rip Van Winkle* are among them. Colonial Revival, as it celebrates and evokes the American past, is, in a sense, our autobiography, but a fictional history.

Referring to the houses of Colonial Williamsburg or other eighteenth-century houses as Colonial Revival, as some do, raises the question of whether we are talking about matters of history, memory, or nostalgia. Memory is frequently characterized as personal, while history is more public and collective. Nostalgia is usually defined as a wistful, often excessively sentimental attachment to the past, sometimes accompanied by an attempt to revive a golden age.[10] The attempt to re-create or return to older virtues strikes a chord in many individuals, though most Americans would quail at the thought of having to return to the living conditions of the eighteenth century. Memory is both personal and collective;

there are certain elements that belong to and help shape the individual, just as there is the more public memory or history that is shared by many.[11] History, on one level, is what historians do; they take the past and (hopefully) by interpretation provide some meaning. However, interpretations do change; the actual causes of the Revolutionary War or Thomas Jefferson's relationship with Sally Hemmings, for instance, remain controversial topics. Similarly, the connection of American colonial housing to that of England is much-contested territory. The various forms of Colonial Revival are interpretations of the past, and while the accuracy of these interpretations can be debated, the more important issue is public perception.

Although there are many competing forces and fads in the public consciousness, such as the current nostalgic interest in mid-twentieth-century modernism or the Arts and Crafts movement, a fundamental core of the American memory views the colonial period as the bedrock for an American idiom. How true this is remains open to question, but history is in many ways a fable agreed upon. Also important is the question of just whose history we are honoring. The African-American and native-American view of the colonial period may be very different from the European-American view. Perceptions of history are constantly changing.

Pitot House, New Orleans, 1799–1805. Entrance facade.

In spite of the long-lived popularity of Colonial Revival, many individuals continue to be suspicious of the integrity of the idiom as applied to the American house. Many architects, architectural critics, and commentators have condemned it as banal and outmoded, announcing its death repeatedly since its beginnings in the nineteenth century. Frank Lloyd Wright found what he called the "Colonial pretense" to be "foolish," characterizing such houses as "ribald and inebriate freaks of fashion bedecked with painful deformities."[12] Architecture critic Lewis Mumford once said that Colonial Revival "has precious little to do with a living architecture."[13] Despite claims by some historians that Colonial Revival was exclusively a nineteenth- and early-twentieth-century phenomenon, it consumed most of the American architectural discourse of the twentieth century and threatens to do the same in the twenty-first.

Must American architecture and art be strictly of the present time, or may they also draw from the past? Part of the issue revolves around questions of what is American. Another concern is the question of authenticity and whether the past can still be communicated through imitation.[14] Like most historical issues, there can be a multiplicity of answers and we can draw many conclusions. Colonial Revival contains a reactionary element, but themes such as innovation and accommodation to the latest technology run through aspects of the Colonial Revival house. The modern versus Colonial Revival debate contains firmly entrenched positions that take no prisoners and, like most hard-line arguments, it is composed of a combination of reality and illusion, a few facts and many myths. In America, a tension exists between the new and the past, or what we now call "modernity versus history." This characteristic appeared very early in this country's history and continues unabated today. But in the early twenty-first century, the Colonial Revival thrives.

Colonial Revival invites parody, which is an aspect of its story that I have tried to guard against. A born modernist and an admirer of modern art, architecture, and furniture, I have realized as a historian that many Americans remain uncomfortable with, and frequently loathe, modernist design, preferring Colonial Revival. This is not to say that they are right and I am wrong but to realize that to ignore Colonial Revival, which has existed for nearly two centuries, is to gloss over a great deal of man-made America.

This book is divided into four chapters spanning the Colonial Revival house's antecedents, discovery, triumph, and status since World War II. To some degree, the choice of dates such as the Civil War, or 1910, or World War II, are arbitrary—a means of organizing information. Nothing completely stops or starts at a date such as 1910; older attitudes

Charles Addams, "The Remodeled House," printed in *The New Yorker*, 1946.

and styles continue, and the roots of the new were laid years prior. However, one can claim that within the date range, certain commonalities exist and offer a means of understanding the different house types, styles, and attitudes involved. The houses chosen, however selective, are representative of Colonial Revival, indicating to varying depths its range stylistically, socially, geographically, and chronologically.

The Colonial Revival story is not simple and straightforward, but contains many twists, turns, and ambiguities, not unlike a composition by Charles Ives, who, in spite of being declared a prophet of modernism, had some Colonial Revival tendencies. His *Symphony No. 2* is similar to the multilayered character and abstruseness of the Colonial Revival phenomenon. Or another musical analogy might be Rodgers and Hammerstein teaming up with Philip Glass to create a Broadway production of folksy good cheer celebrating the American past with ominous low sounds in the background. History, the past, is always open to new interpretations or redesigns. Colonial Revival remains an unfinished symphony.

Explorations

1781 TO THE CIVIL WAR

Thomas Jefferson, writing in 1781, characterized Virginia's colonial houses as "very rarely constructed of stone or brick, much the greater portion being of scantling and boards, plaster with lime. It is impossible to devise things more ugly, uncomfortable, and happily more perishable." He gave faint praise to the Capitol at Williamsburg but condemned all else: "The genius of architecture seems to have shed its maledictions over this land." Jefferson concluded, "Every half century then our country becomes a *tabula rasa,* whereon we have to set out anew." Sixty years later, author Louisa Tuthill wrote, in an early history of American architecture, that early New England buildings possessed an "uncouth style," dismissing them as "wooden enormities." Tuthill echoed Jefferson: the early buildings of the colonists lacked taste, they were not models for imitation.[1] Such devastating commentary has led many historians to claim that interest in colonial architecture and its revival was nonexistent before the Civil War.

However, in the eight decades between the Revolution and the Civil War, a few individuals began to explore the American colonial past, and attitudes emerged that would impact later generations. For instance, Thomas Jefferson's tendency to discard the past for new beginnings shifted slightly in the 1820s, when he advocated that the house in Philadelphia where he wrote the Declaration of Independence might serve as a shrine and be preserved. Certainly one cannot claim that there existed a full-fledged Colonial Revival

John Hartwell Cocke, Bremo Recess, Fluvanna County, Virginia, 1834–36
(renovation to original house built 1807–8). Entrance facade.

with major public support, but certain buildings and monuments were created that indicated a nascent interest in reproducing elements of the colonial past. Americans, under the sway of nationalism and looking for the safety of history, began to explore, preserve, and, in selected cases, reproduce Early American buildings. Equally important was the identification of key motifs, personalities, and events that would provide touchstones for the Colonial Revival of the future. The results would be buildings such as the new steeple on Independence Hall; Longfellow's house in Cambridge, Massachusetts; Washington Irving's Sunnyside, in Tarrytown, New York; John Hartwell Cocke's Bremo Recess, in Fluvanna County, Virginia; the rescue of Mount Vernon in Fairfax County, Virginia; and a flood of statues, paintings, and books that would celebrate America's colonial past.[2]

NATIONALISM AND STYLE

Behind this exploration of the colonial past existed the greater international context to which Americans were responding. The invention of the modern nation-state in the eighteenth century created a need for bonding and loyalty among citizens tied to the country and a casting off of royal or ecclesiastical roots. A national consciousnesses, or patriotism, and a devotion to one's country above all others, endowing it with special traits and destiny, sometimes bordering on the divine, is a necessity of the modern nation-state. Nationalism is, in a sense, invented, examples of which include celebrations such as Independence Day in the United States, Bastille Day in France, and Guy Fawkes Day in England. In 1807, Virginians held a "jubilee" to commemorate the initial settlement at Jamestown.[3]

Nationalism led architecture in several directions during this period, including what came to be called "associationism" and the invention of style. On the one hand, there was the associative value of architecture—the glory of Greece or Rome equated with the latest accomplishments of Britain or the United States. But this implied that there was such a thing as a definable national image or style. Until around 1750, in architecture *style* meant the columnar orders: Doric, Ionic, and Corinthian. Gradually it evolved to mean definable types of architecture as characterized by ornament, form, or construction, and native to certain geographical areas. [4] Thomas Rickman's book *An Attempt to Discriminate the Styles of English Architecture* (1817) and Heinrich Hubsch's *In welchem Style solen wir bauen?* [In What Style Should We Build?] (1828), and many more throughout the nineteenth century, categorized the various styles and made arguments concerning their appropriateness. The so-called battle of the styles began,

resulting in the appearance of a bewildering number of revivals—Greek, Roman, Gothic and/or Medieval, Italianate, and Renaissance, in addition to the more tangential Oriental, Japanese, Viking, and Islamic—across Europe, the United States, and, ultimately, Africa and Asia. The suitability of these revival styles versus the quest for a modern style became one of the mainstays of architectural debate and practice for the next two centuries and beyond.

Integral to the notion of style was the concept that a building's appearance conveyed meaning and acted as a communicator, capable of conferring status and influencing or inspiring behavior. Size, whether large or small, materials, and function were important elements, but more important was that style and ornament could convey messages, both literal and subliminal. The messages might include associations with the great accomplishments of the past, or relationships with the landscape, or expressions of modernity.

The concept of style as a carrier of nationalistic ideology grew out of the belief that architecture and art provided an index to a country's stature, morality, and, of course, taste. Augustus W. N. Pugin (1812–52), the English Gothic revivalist argued: "God . . . has implanted a love of nation and country in every man . . . national feeling and national architecture are at so low an ebb, that it becomes an absolute duty in every Englishman to attempt their revival."[5] A few years later, English critic John Ruskin, writing in *The Seven Lamps of Architecture* (1849)—what became the most popular book on architecture in the nineteenth century—summarized: "It has been my endeavor to show in the proceeding pages how every form of noble architecture is in some sort the embodiment of the Polity, Life, History, and Religious faith of nations." Ruskin's claim that a nation's architecture expressed morality found a large following in the United States well into the twentieth century.[6]

Pugin and Ruskin occupied one extreme in the argument, but even modest observations expressed similar sentiments. Owen Jones, in his book *The Grammar of Ornament* (1856), which would become a mainstay of all architectural offices, wrote as "Proposition 2" in his "General Principles": "Architecture is the material expression of the wants, the faculties, and the sentiments of the age in which it is created."[7] This belief that architecture carried meaning resulted in most Western countries going through revivalist debates as they attempted to identify a style (or styles) from their past that represented their national origins and agendas. Hence in England in the 1830s, the Decorated Gothic was deemed appropriate and used for the Houses of Parliament. France veered between a variety of classical idioms ranging from the mansards of the Louvre, to the overboiled Baroque derived from Louis XIV as at the Paris Opera, or medieval sources as advocated by French architect and writer Eugéne-Emmanuel Viollet-le-Duc. Viollet-le-Duc argued: "Each nation, or to speak more correctly, each center of civilization . . . has a genius of its own which must not be disregarded; and it is because during the last three centuries we have too often failed to appreciate our own genius, that our arts . . . have become hybrid."[8] The Gothic for him was the only true French style. The same type of national style debate took place in Sweden, Russia, Italy, Germany, Hungary, and almost every Western European country. This search for a national style occurred not just in architecture, but also had analogies in history, painting, gardening, statuary, the decorative arts, and novels and poetry.

Popularly known as the youngest of nations, the United States needed a history and an identity. One popular solution was the notion of investing meaning in the landscape of the new country. Instead of the man-made monuments of European history, the United States offered nature and the wonders of the new world such as Niagara Falls in New York and the Natural Bridge in Virginia. This American exceptionalism, or the concept of the uniqueness and divine ordination of the United States, was a byproduct of hubris, pride, and ignorance (few Americans really knew Europe), and a consequence of the country's having a large inferiority complex. The questions of whether America had a history worthy of study, and an American art and architecture that could flourish, remained debatable well into the twentieth century.

EXHUMING AMERICA'S PAST

A few Americans deplored the country's lack of history and set about to provide it with a public memory. In 1817, the United States Congress commissioned John Trumbull to create a cycle of historical paintings based on his earlier work for the rotunda at the United States Capitol. By 1826, Trumbull had installed in the Capitol four large canvases that depicted important events such as the Declaration of Independence, the British surrender at Yorktown, and the resignation of George Washington. In the mid-1820s, sculptural panels of Pocahontas, Captain John Smith, the landing of the pilgrims, and other early events were also added, followed by the addition of more history paintings in the period 1840–1855.[9] Of course the 1820s marked the fiftieth anniversary of the American Revolution; 1820 marked the 200th anniversary of the landing of pilgrims at Plymouth Rock, also the year that the Pilgrim Society was founded. The year 1825 marked the fiftieth anniversary of the Battle of Bunker Hill, and, consequently, a large monument was projected, though its actual design came in 1832 and its completion in 1842.

Independence Hall, Philadelphia, Pennsylvania, north facade after restoration, ca. 1846. Woodcut by Robert Sears, from *Pictorial Description of the United States* (1848).

In the 1820s, a search for a tangible past brought Independence Hall in Philadelphia under scrutiny. Also known as the Pennsylvania State House, it had served as the site of the signing of the Declaration of Independence in 1776, the site of the Constitutional Convention in 1787, and was the first United States Capitol. By 1781, the wood-frame steeple of the tower (on the south side) had rotted; it was then torn down and replaced by a low cap. Seeking to commemorate the important events of the 1770s and to distinguish Philadelphia's skyline, the city council commissioned William Strickland, an eminent Philadelphia architect, to design the steeple. Strickland produced two schemes. His first, a tall brick tower, caused concern, as it did not follow the original structure. Strickland's second design, in wood, was erected in 1828. At 164 feet, the new steeple stood much taller than the original 120-foot structure, and its design was more classical than the original. Its progression of parts, from the square wood base to a series of plinths on which the two-stage cupola sat, was more in the Christopher Wren–Baroque mode and illuminates one of the enduring themes of the Colonial Revival as it would develop: reinterpret—and improve upon—the past.[10]

Many writers bemoaned the country's lack of a past. Nathaniel Hawthorne once characterized the United States as "a country where there is no shadow, no antiquity, no mystery, no picturesque and gloomy wrong, nor anything but a commonplace prosperity, in a broad and simple daylight."[11] Various authors tried to remedy this deficiency of antiquity by writing fiction set in a historical American background. James Fenimore Cooper's *The Spy* (1821) and the "Leatherstocking Tales" (1823–41) utilized the eighteenth century as a setting and in the process helped invent the archetypal male American hero—a loner beyond the pale of civilization. Nathaniel Hawthorne found inspiration in his Salem, Massachusetts, background for his novels *The Scarlet Letter* (1850) and *The House of the Seven Gables* (1851). Others such as William Gilmore Simms, a Southern novelist, and William Cullen Bryant, the New York editor and poet of nature who also wrote historical poetry such as "Marion's Men" and "The Battle-Field" helped invent a fictitious American past.

LONGFELLOW AND THE VASSALL-CRAIGIE HOUSE, CAMBRIDGE, MASSACHUSETTS

Impacted by the Finnish epic *Kalevala,* Henry Wadsworth Longfellow became the American Homer, creating a fictious past with such poems as "The Skeleton In Armor" (1841), "Evangeline"(1845–47), "The Song of Hiawatha" (1855), "The Courtship of Miles Standish" (1858), "The Midnight Ride of Paul Revere" (1860), and more. Longfellow's sole novel, *Kavanagh* (1849), illuminates the question of the source of an American art. One character, a Mr. Hathaway, claims, "We want a national literature altogether shaggy and unshorn, that

Vassall-Craigie-Longfellow House, Cambridge, Massachusetts, 1759. Entrance hall.

shall shake the earth, like a herd of buffalos." His opponent, a Mr. Churchill, argues, "Westward from hand to hand we pass the lighted torch, but it was lighted at the old domestic fireside of England."[12] Longfellow's poems combined the literary forms and sentiments of England with historical American subjects.

Most of Longfellow's major poems on the American past were written at his Cambridge, Massachusetts, house, the venerable Vassall-Craigie-Longfellow House. Dating to 1759, the house was large with ornate interiors and well known for its Ionic pilasters and large pediment on its street facade. George Washington resided in the house from 1775 to 1776. Longfellow rented a room there in the summer of 1837; after his marriage to Francis Appleton in 1841, his father-in-law purchased the house for the young couple. Longfellow lived in the house until his death in 1882. The Washington connection was one of the reasons Longfellow desired the house, and in the front hall he placed a copy of French artist Jean Antoine Houdon's bust of Washington along with other memorabilia. The importance of the Washington connection comes forth in a poem written for his son:

> Once, ah, once within these walls,
> One whom memory oft recalls,
> The Father of his Country dwelt.[13]

Another poem, "The Old Clock on the Stairs" (1845–46), was originally inspired by a visit to Francis Appleton's ancestral home in Pittsfield, Massachusetts—with its "old-fashioned

"Clock on the Stairs," from *The Poetical Works of Henry Wadsworth Longfellow* (1899).

Vassall-Craigie-Longfellow House. Entrance, south facade.

country seat," "its antique portico," and the tall case clock ("Half-way up the stairs it stands")—but was written in the Cambridge house. The poem inspired succeeding generations of antique-hunting Americans to place their tall case clock on the staircase. Longfellow himself moved the bust of Washington down from the landing, describing it in a letter of 1877: "In his place you will see an Old Dutch Clock, whose silver chimes will lull you to sleep at night."[14]

Longfellow also wrote the "The Courtship of Miles Standish" (1858), which popularized the spinning wheel as an emblem of early Pilgrim culture. The character Priscilla Alden is represented by Longfellow:

> Seated beside her wheel, and the carded wool like a
>   snow-drift
> Piled at her knee, her white hands feeding the ravenous
>   spindle,
> While with her foot on the treadle she guided the wheel....

BELOW: Vassall-Craigie-Longfellow House. Front parlor.

RIGHT: Vassall-Craigie-Longfellow House. Rear parlor.

THE MAGNOLIA

From the days of George Washington to the present time, the colonial type of residence has always been popular. It has housed the greatest figures in American history, science and literature. Many will recognize a close resemblance in the Magnolia to the famous residence at Cambridge, Mass., where the poet Longfellow composed his immortal works. Leading architectural authorities declare that this type will continue to win favor for hundreds of years. There can be no question of its imposing appearance, graceful lines and other attractive features.

"The Magnolia," from the Sears Roebuck Company *Book of Modern Homes* (1921).

Longfellow's poem brought the spinning wheel into the parlor and other rooms of the American house where it became a subject of art. His two daughters, Edith and Annie, added one to their bedroom hearth sometime between 1868 and 1871.[15]

Longfellow elaborated on the house's Colonial features by installing balustrades and placing Colonial architectural fragments in the garden. He had the garden redesigned in a pattern his wife likened to a "Persian rug." Although the design lacked historical credibility and followed mid-nineteenth-century taste, Longfellow's embellishments, particularly his placement of seats where he imagined Washington had sat, endowed it with history. Longfellow's residence at the already well-known house made it even more of an American icon. The house was repeatedly illustrated and described in magazines and books. A visitor around 1852 observed: "Within, iconoclastic innovation has not been allowed to enter with its mallet and trowel, to mar the work of the ancient builder, and to cover with the vulgar stucco of modern art the carved cornices and paneled wainscots."[16]

The house's iconic status continued after Longfellow's death. His daughter enhanced certain features and commissioned Martha Brooks Hutchinson to redesign the garden and

RIGHT, TOP: Washington Irving and George Harvey, Sunnyside, Tarrytown, New York, 1835, 1847 (remodeling and additions to original house built ca. 1783). Entrance facade.

RIGHT, BOTTOM: Sunnyside. West porch.

OVERLEAF: Sunnyside.

add several architectural elements, including a Colonial Revival pergola/summer house. Even later, landscape architect Ellen Shipman worked on the planting plan. All of these redesigns became touchstones for the Colonial Revival garden. The house became one of the most widely copied New England buildings, making it into the Sears, Roebuck and Company's mail order houses catalog under the name of the "Magnolia." The name change came about because Sears added a giant portico that was usually associated with the South, but the advertising copy claimed: "Many will recognize a close resemblance in the Magnolia to the famous residence at Cambridge, Mass., where the poet Longfellow composed his immortal works." Already a shrine, the actual house was opened to the public by Longfellow's family in the early twentieth century. Since 1972, the National Park Service has maintained the house.[17]

WASHINGTON IRVING'S SUNNYSIDE, TARRYTOWN, NEW YORK

Washington Irving, another early literary figure with architectural interests, helped create Dutch Colonial New York

City with his first book, *A History of New York* (1809), written under the pen name Dietrich Knickerbocker, from which the popular New York nickname comes. He later explained: "I hailed my native city as fortunate above all other American cities in having antiquity thus extending back into the regions of doubt and fable." Irving wanted to "embody the traditions . . . in an amusing form" through the employment of "imaginative and whimsical associations."[18] His later work, *The Sketch Book of Geoffrey Crayon, Gent* (1819–20), contained the colonial-based historical burlesques "The Legend of Sleepy Hollow" and "Rip Van Winkle."

In 1835, having already visited Sir Walter Scott at his Medieval Revival confection, Abbotsford, and Lord Byron's Newstead Abbey, Irving purchased a two-room tenant farmhouse, dating to about 1783, on the banks of the Hudson River at Tarrytown, New York. Irving consulted with at least one architect prior to engaging the artist George Harvey to help him remodel and add to the house, which he named Sunnyside. He described his intentions as "to make a little nookery somewhat in the Dutch style, quaint, but unpretending." Speaking of the house in a letter to Harvey, Irving noted, "I observe in some designs of old buildings a mixture of gables with 'crow steps' and projecting eves." At Sunnyside, Harvey and Irving added stepped gables, which had a Dutch ancestry, along with clustered chimneys, and other details. "I have repaired and renovated it with religious care, in the genuine Dutch style and have adorned and illustrated it with sundry relics of the glorious days of the New Netherlands," Irving said of the house. Irving added the fictional date of 1656 to the west side of the house and, over the front door, a tablet inscribed with the words "Geo. Harvey, Boumr."—which is the abbreviation for *bouwmeester,* or architect, in Dutch. In 1847, a tower described as being in the Spanish style was added. Unfortunately, the modern age intruded, and by 1850 Irving felt bothered by the noise from the nearby railroad along the river.[19]

BELOW: Sunnyside. South entrance.

OPPOSITE: Sunnyside. West gable showing fictitious date of construction.

OVERLEAF: Sunnyside.

ABOVE: Sunnyside. Dining room.

BELOW, LEFT: Sunnyside. Irving's bedroom.

BELOW, RIGHT: Sunnyside. Front guest room.

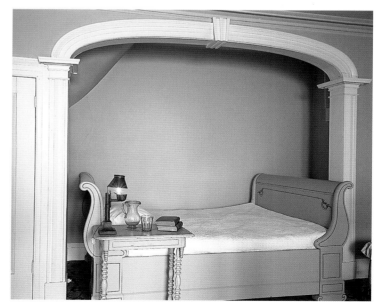

Admired by Andrew Jackson Downing and included in one of his domestic architecture guidebooks, Sunnyside immediately became famous and visited. Pictured endlessly in books, articles, and travel literature, Irving's Sunnyside was not only a literary shrine for Americans, but also a means of appropriating the past. A writer for *Harper's* saw in Sunnyside "a wonderfully unique little edifice, totally unlike any thing else in our land, but always calling up our remembrances or our fancies of merrie rural England, with a hint here or there of its old Dutch leaven." The writer added: "In his own serio-comic description of his home, Mr. Irving speaks of it as being 'one of the oldest edifices for its size in the whole country;' and as, 'though of small dimensions, yet, like many small people of mightily spirit, valuing itself greatly upon its antiquity.'" Although various visitors noted that Irving had manufactured certain elements such as the weather vanes, the house's authenticity was never doubted, for as one visitor to Sunnyside exclaimed: "Here, was no castle in the air, but a realized daydream." In a manner not dissimilar to Scott's Abbotsford, Irving, through remodeling and careful selection of objects, produced a fictional rendering of the past that seemed authentic to most visitors.[20]

BREMO RECESS AND OTHER EXPLORATIONS

In Fluvanna County, Virginia, a remodeling similar to Irving's took place at the Bremo Plantation. There, from 1834 to 1836, General George Hartwell Cocke, a former associate of Thomas Jefferson and the owner of the very Jeffersonian Upper Bremo (1817–20), remodeled an existing house. Cocke,

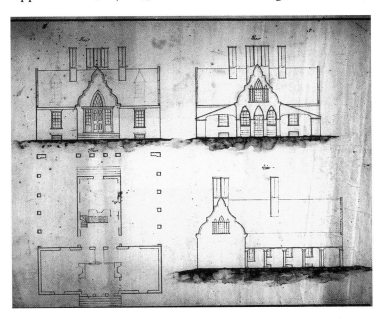

John Hartwell Cocke, Bremo Recess, Fluvanna County, Virginia, 1834–36 (renovation to original house built 1807–8). Drawing showing renovation elevations and plan.

Bremo Recess. Outbuilding, ca. 1836.

probably with the assistance of an anonymous builder/designer, encased the house, called Bremo Recess, with a brick Jacobean Tudor–style projecting facade, its gables featuring the appropriate curves and crow steps. Triple-pointed arch openings were employed on the porch, and clustered columnar chimney stacks enlivened the roof. In a letter of 1844, Cocke stated that "the stile [sic] is copied from the only two specimens of the like buildings I ever saw—the well remembered old Six-chimney House in Wmsburg . . . and Bacons [sic] Castle."[21] The house in Williamsburg to which he referred was long gone but Bacon's Castle (ca. 1665), also known as the Arthur Allen House, in Tidewater, Virginia, one of the earliest and most historic sites, was already well known. For his design of Bremo Recess, Cocke drew upon Bacon's Castle's stepped and curved-end elevations and clustered chimneys.

As examples of houses done in the Colonial Revival idiom, Bremo Recess and Sunnyside appear to be unique for their time. However, there are other buildings that demonstrate that architects were looking at the American past for design inspiration. Arthur Gilman's Arlington Street Unitarian Church (1860) in Boston revived the Gibbs-Wren style that had been popular in eighteenth-century New England. Gilman had written admiringly of Early American architecture, the Early American church in particular, in an article published in

North American Review in April 1844. Gilman also utilized the colonial image for a new town hall at Exeter, New Hampshire, in 1855.[22] Newport, Rhode Island, which would play a very important role in the post–Civil War stage of Colonial Revival, received its first duplication of a colonial-era structure in 1858 at the Redwood Library, where the Boston architect George Snell copied Peter Harrison's original design.

WASHINGTON AND MOUNT VERNON

The various commemorations of George Washington serve as an index to America's changing attitudes toward the past.[23] Jean Antoine Houdon's sculpture *George Washington* (1785–91) in the Virginia State Capitol, which portrays Washington as a Cincinnatus figure complete with a plow and sword, was clearly a contemporary work. Later depictions of Washington, as in the *Washington Monument* (1815–42) in Baltimore, or Horatio Greenough's *Washington* (1832–41), originally intended for the United States Capitol, or the *Washington Monument* (1845–84) in Washington, D. C., remove him from his historical context and abstract his memory into renditions such as Trajan's Column, a gowned Greco-Roman law giver and an obelisk. In the 1850s, Washington's image underwent another change, this time to become a historical figure. Part of the shift in Washington's portrayal came from the increasing sectional tensions between the North and the South. At Union Square in New York on July 4, 1856, an equestrian *Washington* by Henry Kirke Brown was unveiled, while in Richmond another *Washington,* this one by Thomas Crawford, who placed Washington on horseback and surrounded him by Virginia worthies, was unveiled in 1858. Emanuel Leutze's *Washington Crossing the Delaware* (1851) remains the best known of many paintings done in the period. Thomas Pritchard Rossiter and Louis Mignet's *Washington and Lafayette at Mt. Vernon, 1784* (1859) helped to put him into an architectural context.

The 1850s also signaled attention directed to actual buildings associated with Washington. On July 4, 1850, General Winfield Scott came up the Hudson River to raise the flag over the Hasbrouck House at Newburgh, New York. A simple farmhouse — originally erected in 1724 and enlarged several times between 1750 and 1753 and again in 1770 — it served as Washington's headquarters from 1782 to 1783, the last years

LEFT: Bremo Recess.

OVERLEAF: George Washington, Mount Vernon, Fairfax County, Virginia, ca. 1735, 1758–63, 1774–87, and later restorations. View from Potomac River.

Hasbrouck House, Newburgh, New York. Drawing by Stanford White, ca. 1876.

of the Revolution. (Earlier in 1850, before Scott's arrival at Hasbrouck House, the New York State Legislature had voted—after a protracted battle—to allocate funds to purchase Hasbrouck House, making it the first historic house museum in the United States).[24] Its interest to architects is revealed in an 1875 sketch by Stanford White that focuses on the huge and long sloping roof, which fed into the image of Early American houses as salt boxes.

Washington died in 1799, and over the course of the next half-century his home, Mount Vernon, would become a patriotic Mecca and shrine. During his lifetime, Washington had altered, added to, and redesigned Mount Vernon on numerous occasions. Although Mount Vernon remained in family hands, it deteriorated, and the threat to put it on the "public market" brought pressure for its preservation. Ann Pamela Cunningham of Charleston, South Carolina, stepped forward in 1853 and broadcast an appeal, initially to women of the South, and later nationwide, to raise the $200,000 the Washington heirs required. Over the next five years she attempted various methods to secure the house, finally saving it by organizing the Mount Vernon Ladies Association. The famous orator and former senator from Massachusetts Edward Everett embarked on a speaking campaign for the association and donated his considerable lecture fees to the ladies.[25] With Everett's assistance

and proceeds from other fundraising efforts, Cunningham was able to secure the amount needed to acquire the house.

Everett's talks contained patriotic appeal and also an enduring theme of the Colonial Revival attitude as it developed: The houses of the colonialists exhibited modesty and a "noble simplicity." His oration described Blenheim in England, built for the Duke of Marlborough, as "all that old could buy, or the bounty of his own or foreign princes could bestow, or taste devise, or art execute, or ostentation would lavish." In contrast stood Mount Vernon, about which he said: "It boasts no spacious portal nor gorgeous colonnade, nor mosey elevation, nor storied tower. The porter's lodge at Blenheim Castle, nay the marble dog kennels were not built for the entire cost of Mount Vernon."[26] Although the comparison was apt, Mount Vernon certainly was not chaste with regards to its American contemporaries; indeed, it ranked as one of the most ornate and pretentious houses for its period. Washington had closely directed its elaboration, even while off fighting the British during the American Revolution.

Behind the saving of Mount Vernon lay patriotic zeal and honor to Washington. In the minds of some of the effort's participants, including Cunningham, the house might become a rallying point to save the country from the coming blood bath of the Civil War. Eventually, the house opened to the public. Although the Civil War restricted visitors and brought financial hard times, Mount Vernon had been rescued. Beginning in the 1860s, and continuing the project today, the Mount Vernon Ladies Association directed repairs and restorations to the house with various degrees of fidelity. Already famous, Mount Vernon's popularity only increased as it became the most visited house in America

THE HOME OF WASHINGTON.

Currier and Ives, *The Home of Washington*, ca. 1870, colored lithograph.

and, in time, a model for not just preservation and restoration, but also for new American houses. Mount Vernon, Longfellow's Sunnyside, and Bremo Recess reveal the nascent interest in Early American architecture in the period before the Civil War.

Other stories exist that indicate how Americans, both individually and collectively, began to re-create the past prior to the Civil War. After the conflict, a very different situation existed that pointed to a new future but also created an even more pressing need for a past; the Colonial Revival burst into full flower.

ABOVE: Mount Vernon. West entrance facade.

RIGHT: Mount Vernon. Front parlor.

Discovery and Ascendancy

THE CIVIL WAR TO 1910

Americans identified architecture of the colonial era as a national image between the Civil War and the first decade of the twentieth century. During this time, the contours of American history changed significantly—evolving from a single-minded focus on Washington and a few events to a much wider perspective—as historians, architects, artists, and writers excavated the colonial past. While there were other popular historical styles during this time, prominent among them was the romanticized image of the Early American house, which continued to grow in popularity as a model for the American home.

After the Civil War, the United States grew exponentially and became a world power, politically and commercially. From a population of approximately thirty-two million in 1861, there were more than ninety-two million by 1910. Some of this growth came from the vast numbers of European and Asian immigrants. The need to educate the new immigrants with appropriate American ideals was a subtle yet important element of the new emphasis on United States history and one reason for the popularity of the Colonial Revival style. But America and Americans changed in other ways: Farming—and the rural life in general—began to disappear as Americans piled into and swelled cities. The figures tell the story: in 1860, the percentage of the population classified as urban was just under twenty percent; by 1910, it had grown to 45.5 percent. The expansion, which occurred in the North, the Midwest, and, to a lesser degree

McKim, Mead & White, Isaac Bell House, Newport, Rhode Island, 1881–83.
South entrance facade.

but still significant, in the South, along with the settling of the rest of the country and the so-called closing of the frontier in 1890, helped to trigger a nostalgic look at the colonial past.

One indication of the changing opinion toward the buildings of America's past was the address the president of the American Institute of Architects (AIA), Richard Mitchell Upjohn, gave in 1869 praising colonial-era public buildings and houses in New York and New England. Near the end of his talk, Upjohn observed: "May we not gain a valuable lesson while contemplating these works of our forefathers? Old and quaint as they are, will we not see by comparing them with the works of our own hands that their authors regarded the law of harmony between a building and its surroundings better than we do at the present day?"[1] Given that Upjohn created several very large High Victorian Gothic buildings such as the Connecticut State Capitol (1875–78) in Hartford, such comments might come as a surprise. But one senses Upjohn's uneasiness with regard to what future generations might think of post–Civil War architecture.

A similar appreciation came from the Boston Society of Architects, who held a meeting in 1869 during which the work of Charles Bulfinch (1763–1844) was given high praise. Later in that year, William R. Emerson gave a "sermon" bemoaning the destruction of old England houses, which he called "the only truly American architecture." The controversial destruction in 1863 of the John Hancock House on Boston's Beacon Hill had raised the level of historical consciousness among architects.[2] These homages to colonial-era architecture embodied criticisms of contemporary design and indicated a concern among some American architects: Gothic-towered and mansard-roofed structures were being created for the Gilded Age, but something appeared to be wrong.

THE DISCOVERIES OF CHARLES McKIM AND ROBERT PEABODY

In the mid-1870s, two young architects—one from Boston, Robert Peabody, a partner in the firm Peabody & Stearns, the other from New York, Charles McKim, eventually of the firm McKim, Mead & White—emerged as the major polemicists for a Colonial Revival. Both had recently returned from study in Paris at the Ecole des Beaux-Arts and were acutely aware of the architecture of the contemporary Aesthetic movement and the Queen Anne Revival in Great Britain, which spurred them to look closely at early New England houses.

To American architects such as McKim, the British Queen Anne Revival led them to investigate their own architectural heritage. The English Queen Anne contained many features, the small paned leaded-glass windows, the clustered chimneys, the exposed interior beams, the plaster decorated ceilings, the molded brickwork, the hanging tiles, the classical details that could be seen on older houses in New England and the middle Atlantic states. Another element of this new English architecture that McKim would have noted was the living room, or great hall, of the English country houses, which acted as the spatial and organizing center of the house.

Back in the United States, in 1870, McKim worked for H. H. Richardson, and while in his employ visited Newport, Rhode Island. In 1874 he married Annie Bigelow, whose family owned a large house on the waterfront near many eighteenth-century houses. McKim began to examine Newport's colonial heritage, publishing his findings in the *New York Sketch Book of Architecture*. Although Richardson was listed as editor on the introductory page of the periodical, Montgomery Schuyler, a member of the staff, noted that the real force was the de facto editor, Charles McKim, whom he recalled as having "naturally used the publication to promulgate his own essays."[3] Primarily composed of plates with a small amount of descriptive text, the *New York Sketch Book,* like its sister publication in Boston, the *Architectural Sketch Book,* was addressed to the professional architect, not the builder. In their introduction, Richardson and McKim stated their intention "to do a little toward the much-needed task of preserving some record of the early architecture of our country, now fast disappearing." They asked for sketches "of the beautiful, quaint, and picturesque features, which belong to so many buildings, now almost disregarded, of our Colonial and Revolutionary period."[4]

Old House in Newport (1874), Bishop George Berkeley House, Middletown, Rhode Island, ca. 1729.

Entranced with colonial-era architecture and decorative arts, McKim hired a photographer in 1874 to record Newport's treasures, and he presented bound plates to clients and friends. One of McKim's photographs, of Whitehall (1729), also known as the Bishop Berkeley House, in Middleton, Rhode Island, appeared in the December 1874 issue of the *Sketch Book.* In the accompanying text McKim called for more than an antiquarian recitation of facts: "Now let somebody write about them as 'Architecture.' The Architects are their true historians." He admired the "picturesque surroundings and architectural merit of many of these old buildings," and backhandedly complimented them by observing that they were not "ugly," or "at least they are never aggressively so, like so many of their modern neighbors."[5] The photograph showed the picturesque rear with the textured sweeping roof that became a major motif of many succeeding houses designed by McKim and others.

A similar attitude toward the informal qualities of shelter, quaintness, and the picturesque in Early American architecture can be seen in Stanford White's drawing of Washington's headquarters at Newburgh, New York, published in a later issue of the *New York Sketch Book.* Also appearing were illustrations of more formal eighteenth-century architecture. [6] Until the mid-1880s, the informal, or vernacular, aspect of architecture of the colonial era proved to be of most interest to McKim and other American architects. But, by the mid-1880s, this aspect was supplanted by the more formal eighteenth-century Georgian style.

McKim's first attempt at Colonial Revival was the remodeling of the "Quaker" Tom Robinson House in Newport (1874–75). An imposing gambrel-roofed structure on the water side of Washington Street, the house had been built around 1725, with later additions in 1760, and had served as the headquarters of the Vicomte de Noailles in the American Revolution. In 1874, a Robinson descendant, Benjamin R. Smith, asked McKim to add a kitchen wing and convert the original keeping room that overlooked the bay into a rear sitting room with an exterior porch. In the sitting room, McKim reproduced moldings, paneling, and shutters from the eighteenth-century portion of the house. A photograph published in the *New York Sketch Book* showed the features of the chimney typical of the colonial era—the purple and white Dutch tiles, the mantel shelf, and McKim's more whimsical interpretations such as the finials. From the photograph, the rooms appear snug and low, but actually McKim had inserted windows in the opposite walls, permitting the entrance considerable light, and the hearth was much larger than most sitting room examples from the eighteenth century.[7]

In the next several years, McKim alone—and then in partnership with William R. Mead, and briefly with his brother-in-law William Bigelow, and, after 1879, with Stanford White— merged Queen Anne with colonial-era details to create the "modernized colonial," later christened the "Shingle Style."[8] Mead remembered it this way: "In our early days all of us had a great interest in Colonial architecture, and in 1877 we made what we afterwards called our 'celebrated' trip to New England, for the purpose of visiting Marblehead, Salem, Newburyport and Portsmouth. . . .We made sketches and measured drawings of many of the important Colonial houses . . . these must represent some of the earliest records of the Colonial period through native drawings."[9] Contemporary critics saw McKim's work as a melding of influences. Clarence Cook, writing in *Scribner's* on contemporary interiors, took note of McKim's Robinson House: "Whatever was added kept true to the spirit of the old time, though without any antiquarian slavishness."[10]

Leading the Boston recovery and celebration of colonial architecture was Robert Peabody, John Hubbard Sturgis, and Arthur Little. Sturgis, a member of an old Boston family, had worked as an architect in England in the 1850s and, consequently, most of his work in Boston and elsewhere followed the High Victorian Gothic of that period. But he became enamored of Early American architecture and in 1863 made perhaps the first set of measured drawings of a colonial house. Sturgis's drawings of the Hancock House (1737) on Beacon Hill prior to its demolition became a major source for later designs.

Peabody trained at the Ecole des Beaux-Arts and returned to Boston in 1870, well aware of the nationalistic implications

Charles Follen McKim, Quaker Tom Robinson House, Newport, Rhode Island, interior remodeling 1874–75. Sitting room fireplace and mantel.

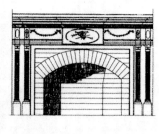
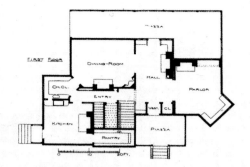

Peabody & Stearns, Denny House, Brush Hill, Milton, Massachusetts
1877–78. Illustration from *American Architect* (February 16, 1878).

of historical styles. Like McKim, he came to the Colonial Revival through the Queen Anne. He visited England and the Continent between January and May 1876 and later recalled: "When we began, Victorian Gothic was at its best. You were expected to declare that you belonged to the English Gothic School or to the Classical School, and it was exactly like saying whether you were a Baptist or a heathen."[11] In talks and articles, Peabody argued: "There is no revival so little of an affectation on our soil as that of the beautiful work of the Colonial days. . . . It is our legitimate field for imitation, and we have much of it to study right in our own neighborhood."[12] In another article, in which he signed himself "Georgian," Peabody rhetorically asked, "With our centennial year have we not discovered that we have a past worthy of study?. . . Our Colonial work is our only native source of antiquarian study and inspiration."[13] Peabody's sketches of several New England houses accompanied these articles.

Arthur Little, title page from *Early New England Interiors* (1878).

The first house of Peabody and Stearns's that overtly contained colonial features, the Denny House (1877–78) at Brush Hill, Milton, Massachusetts, possessed a group of intersecting steep gable roofs, which was a feature Peabody identified as particularly colonial. Clapboards covered the exterior and a Palladian window, bay windows, and tall pilasters gave it a Georgian air. The plan, though irregular, could be interpreted as an attempt to meld the central hall of the eighteenth century to a Victorian particularization of function. Inside the house, the "cupboards, mantels and staircases" were "designed after the style of Colonial work."[14]

Peabody and Stearns's office became one of the hubs of the New England Colonial Revival. Drawn to it were young architects such as William E. Barry and Arthur Little. Barry published *Pen Sketches of Old Houses.* The book contained no text but the drawings had evocative titles such as "A fireplace of the Olden time." Barry would establish a career restoring old houses, as well as designing new ones, in southern Maine.[15] Arthur Little's *Early New England Interiors,* which was released approximately four years later, was extremely popular. Some of the book's drawings, including "Little Harbor" on the frontispiece of the book, had been done in the company of Peabody during a tour in July 1877. Little's drawings lacked the atmosphere of Barry's, but with their hard edge and emphasis on detail, the book became a staple of many architects' offices. Little soon opened his own office and began designing resort houses inspired by colonial architecture for wealthy Bostonians. With his later partner, Herbert W. C. Browne, Little's firm did substantial work, such as the Hamilton House in South Berwick, Maine (see page 75). Little and Browne were close friends with another Bostonian architect, Ogden Codman Jr.; they dubbed themselves "the colonial trinity."[16]

OTHER COLONIAL DISCOVERIES

Illuminating the growing interest in the colonial past were George Boughton's *Pilgrims Going to Church* (1867) and Daniel Chester French's *Minute Man,* unveiled at Concord, Massachusetts, in 1875. Along with many writings they indicate the dominance of New England as the center of colonial America.

Another influence in the discovery of colonial-era architecture was the International Centennial Exposition of 1876. Held in Fairmont Park, Philadelphia, the fair contained a variety of patriotic themes, ranging from displays highlighting America's industrial and commercial might, to works that demonstrated a quest for artistic legitimacy and a nod to America's colonial past. Two structures explicitly invoked the colonial theme: the Connecticut state building, which recalled a ca.1700 colonial home; and a building representing Massachusetts named New England Farmer's Home and Modern Kitchen. The latter's intent was to contrast a farmer's log cabin of around 1776 with a modern kitchen. The interior of the log cabin was outfitted with old furniture, hung-dried herbs, and, hanging over the large fireplace, a musket and powder horn. The Massachusetts log cabin was totally fictitious since few, if any, seventeenth- and eighteenth-century New Englanders ever lived in such a structure. Log cabins were actually introduced in the colonial period in the mid-Atlantic states by German and Swedish settlers, and the form eventually spread to other areas. In the nineteenth century, the log cabin became a political emblem of many campaigns and was also pictured by artists such as Thomas Cole and by popular print makers such as Currier and Ives. Although lacking in historical accuracy, the Massachusetts log cabin's emphasis on domestic artifacts was telling and a sign of things to come.

The written works of the period made an important contribution to America's newfound consciousness of its past. Through historical novels such as Sarah Orne Jewett's *The Tory Lover* (1901), which referenced New England, to Thomas Nelson Page's *The Old South* (1891), which focused on Virginia, to Helen Hunt Jackson's *Ramona* (1884), which was set in the West, Americans were transported back into the colonial era. An interest in the colonial past surfaced in architectural house pattern books such as William M. Woollett's *Old Homes Made New* (1878), which lauded an early house: "Although perhaps in a dilapidated condition, its preservation is in the highest degree desirable, owing to the associations of family,

its particular phase or style of architecture, or the historical interest that may attach itself. In this phase of architecture there are many things which are quaint, interesting and, in an artistic light, good." [17]

Support for the colonial idiom as America's national style of architecture came in Boston with the January 1, 1876, appearance of the professional architectural journal *The American Architect and Building News.* The editors, William P. P. Longfellow and William Rotch Ware, felt duty-bound to bring order to American architecture. They believed the "abundance of precedent" meant "for a long time, simply confusion." In subsequent articles, Longfellow and Ware fleshed out the problem: "We have to create an architecture, and we are expected to furnish it ready-made. We are not given three or four centuries to develop it in." One solution included promoting better architectural education and condemning as evil the vernacular builder and pattern books. Various foreign styles would be advocated, but tucked into an array of articles was the colonial style, which received praise for its "great refinement," "elegance," and dignity; it exhibited, as they put it, "the advantages of working in a definite and well-understood style." From the earlier work, an indigenous architectural strength could be derived that the editors felt was missing in most post–Civil War architecture. An English architect summed up much of this sentiment in a letter: "If every American is to become possessed of an historical style, it must spring from the works of the old colonists." [18]

The *American Architect* continued to publish articles on contemporary Colonial Revival designs along with sketches, measured drawings, and photographs of Early American buildings. Many of these articles and illustrations were later reprinted in a mammoth book entitled *The Georgian Period*

INTERIOR OF NEW ENGLAND KITCHEN.

Interior of New England Kitchen, illustration of Massachusetts Annex, Centennial Exhibition, Philadelphia, 1876.

Fairbanks House, Dedham, Massachusetts, ca. 1636 with additions. Illustration from *American Architect and Building News* (November 29, 1881).

(1898–1902).[19] Colonial work also appeared in the newer professional journals such as *The Inland Architect, The Architectural Record, The Brickbuilder,* and others. *The Colonial Architecture of Maryland, Pennsylvania and Virginia* (1892) was compiled by Joseph Everett Chandler, a Boston architect (who will appear again in conjunction with the Stevens–Coolidge House in chapter three) who intended the book's plates to serve "wholly for the use of architects." A reviewer praised the book but noted that the "artistic pictures . . . will interest non-professional book buyers quite as much as it will architects [for] artistic effect."[20] At a more sophisticated level were the architectural histories of Early American architecture, in which architects such as Norman Isham and Albert F. Brown produced detailed histories of early houses, dividing them up into so-called periods and creating a type of organic evolution in which a single-room house became a double room and onwards. Isham emphasized the "scientific" approach, or "accuracy," of the work. They tended to place early dates on the houses, which later historians have disputed, but more important to the wider public was the focus in these volumes on vernacular and handcrafted elements, which were depicted in marvelous drawings of framing elements, hinges, and fireplaces. One consequence of the work of Isham and others like him was the founding in 1910 of the Society for the Preservation of New England Antiquities.[21]

One of the first attempts to surmount the anecdotal and localized history was Montgomery Schuyler's lengthy essay of forty pages and many illustrations for *The Architectural Record* in 1895. Schuyler produced a comprehensive view of colonial and post–Revolutionary War buildings, finding much to praise. Schuyler's work answered, albeit with a backhanded compliment, many of the critics who claimed "there did not exist in the county" in 1784 "a single piece of architecture which, when tried even by the standard of that day, can be called respectable. . . . Even the freaks of the colonial carpenters . . . were gentle and subdued extravagance." In comparison with what followed, which he called the Romantic period, he claimed that colonial-era architecture had "saved us."[22] Schuyler's grudging acceptance of colonial-era architecture indicates the shift that was taking place among architects and critics. Prior to this point, Schuyler had been one of the major supporters of H. H. Richardson and Leopold Eidlitz's design approach, which incorporated medieval-inspired organic architecture, but, as he had come to realize, a new classicism had emerged, one with sources that could be traced to Georgian buildings.[23]

Georgian classicism had important repercussions since it implied connections to England. Edith Wharton and Ogden Codman Jr., in their seminal *The Decoration of Houses* (1897), claimed that the term *colonial* indicated "a vague impression that there existed at that time an American architectural style." Elaborating, they said: "As a matter of fact, 'Colonial' architecture is simply a modest copy of Georgian models."[24] For many architects, this opened the door to utilizing English Georgian forms and details as if they were American. A critic writing about a " 'Colonial House' " by McKim, Mead & White observed: "The American 'colonial' was merely an attenuation under very lean economic conditions of the English 'Georgian,' and the modern 'colonial' house at its best always tends to revert in certain respects to the English prototype." The author went on to claim that the Georgian style in the eighteenth century represented the "rising importance of the business man" and the "well-to-do English Bourgeois" and, hence, was entirely appropriate for American adaptation.[25]

The members of the AIA, at their 1890 convention, again voiced concern about colonial-era buildings, this time speaking about the subject in relation to New York, among other cities, and concluding that a committee should be created for the purpose of ensuring their conservation. The resolution summed up what had become a popular sentiment: "The history of civilization and the world is traced by the character of its buildings and its architecture, and the degree of civilization of peoples is determined by the monuments they have left."[26]

The colonial-era garden also emerged as a subject of interest during this period. Although the gardens of Mount Vernon and other early houses had already been studied, it was during the decades of the 1890s and 1900s that the Colonial Revival garden comes into being. Women were especially important to its rise in popularity, and in 1913 the Garden

Club of America was founded in Germantown, Pennsylvania. The various state branches of the Garden Club frequently became involved in historic preservation projects as well as new gardens. The most important codifier of the Colonial Revival garden, however, was Alice Morse Earle, a New Englander, who wrote a series of books on colonial childhood, customs, and gardens.[27] A prominent feature of most Colonial Revival gardens was a domestic scale, in contrast to the large French and Italian gardens that were sometimes created for American estates. In keeping with that domestic nature, the garden would be close to the house and have carefully defined limits in the form of a wall of wood, brick, or boxwood. In general, the garden would have a geometrical layout with a central axis and, often, a central feature such as a sundial. Architectural embellishments would include gates, arbors, and wooden seats. Paths would frequently be of brick or clamshells. Plantings would be varied but popular, including older shrub and flower stock, and, in an area close to the house, there would be a garden space called the "kitchen" or "dooryard" garden.

The Daughters of the American Revolution, the National Society of Colonial Dames, and the rival Colonial Dames were founded in the early 1890s. These groups primarily had social functions (along with certain xenophobic tendencies), but they also helped in preserving colonial remains. In Virginia, Mary Jeffrey Galt and Cynthia Coleman, upset about the decay and possible destruction of venerable buildings and sites at Jamestown and Williamsburg, formed the Association for the Preservation of Virginia Antiquities in 1888.[28] They provided the model for many later state and regional historic-preservation organizations that helped celebrate the colonial past.

MODERNIZED COLONIAL

By the early 1880s, colonial-related styles were beginning to be acknowledged as a solution to the question of an American style. But what exactly was colonial? McKim, Mead & White's work showed the two major directions: innovative adaptation and more historical recall. By late 1879, when Stanford White returned from Europe and joined McKim and Mead, the firm—which, for a short period, included McKim's brother-in-law, William Bigelow—had completed several houses that laid out the stylistic possibilities.[29]

RIGHT: McKim, Mead & White, Isaac Bell House, Newport, Rhode Island, 1881–83. Entrance.

OVERLEAF: Bell House. East facade.

McKim, Mead & White's Isaac Bell House (1881–83) in Newport, Rhode Island, illuminates the innovative approach to the colonial sources. Known today as "Shingle Style," the house was labeled "a Queen Anne villa" by a Newport newspaper, and, in 1886, George William Sheldon, one of the more knowledgeable critics, described it as "modernized colonial." The various labels indicate the difficulty of identifying what was American. The shingle-clad exterior with the various patterns was by the 1880s seen as an element of the vernacular that dated back to the early settlers of the seventeenth century. Explicitly colonial in style (derived from McKim and partners' 1877 tour of the North Shore and Salem) were the tall twin gables and overhang at the third-floor level, which recalled seventeenth-century examples such as the House of the Seven Gables in Salem. On these gables were placed an oval window and tripartite windows, which, stylistically, had Georgian associations. The tower at the side with the strange bell-like top may be a pun on the name of the owner, but the form recalls an eighteenth-century windmill that McKim had photographed in 1874. At the rear, the shape and roofline of

Bell House. Rear facade.

ABOVE: Bell House. Detail of tower.

BELOW: Bell House. Plan.

OPPOSITE: Bell House. East porch.

the service wing explicitly recalled McKim's photograph of the Bishop Berkeley House.[30]

The "modernized colonial" label, which Sheldon bestowed upon the Bell House, implied something more than just a reference to the past. Far larger than any dwelling from the colonial period, the Bell House—with its large porches that engulfed the first floor and pushed out into a tower at one end of the second floor, its imitation bamboo posts, and Chinese dolphins on the entrance canopy—represented a house of today and of the summer colony. Located on Bellevue Avenue, though the entrance was on the side street, the client, Isaac Bell Jr., earned a living as a New York cotton broker and married the sister of James Gordon Bennett Jr., the owner of the *New York Herald* newspaper. Bennett commissioned McKim, Mead & White to design the Newport Casino in 1879 and probably recommended the firm to Bell, though Bell paid for the house. Its cost on completion in 1883 was $26,500 for the land and $40,937.64 for the house, plus

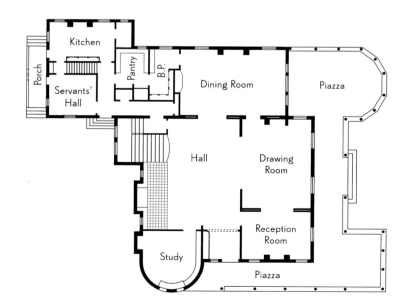

LEFT: Bell House. Dining room.

RIGHT: Bell House. Entrance hall.

BELOW: Bell House. Mantel in reception room.

the cost of the architects' commissions.[31] The needs of a summer resort lifestyle certainly dictated the house's floor plan, with the giant hall measuring thirty by twenty-four feet, the generous openings into the drawing and dining room, and the triple sash windows that gave onto the piazza. Despite the openings and implied freedom of movement, each space had its own particularized decor, which can be generally described as "Aesthetic Movement" with Colonial Revival or classical touches such as swags, rosettes, and sunflowers. The large hearth in the hall was self-consciously colonial in size, and, while the paneling came from Breton bedsteads, the overall intricacy recalled eighteenth-century decor. A prosperous ease was the image the Bell House presented to the world.

The Bell House signifies the careful study made by McKim, Mead & White of the resort lifestyle; as such, it would have many imitators across the United States in the next thirty years. Later, shingles were applied to a variety of building types, from resort hotels to bungalows. But these later examples lack the context of what the Bell House represented at the time. Frank Lloyd Wright summed up how the shingled idiom was viewed in Chicago when he recalled the kidding he took at the Adler and Sullivan office about the house he was erecting in Oak Park in the late 1880s. His original home (and later studio) had a tall peaked roof with a Palladian window, bay windows, and was covered in shingles. His officemates asked him if it was "Seaside or Colonial" in style.[32] Although Wright and others, such as Charles Greene and Henry Greene of Pasadena, California, would eventually condemn the Colonial Revival, one can see in their work lingering influences such as the focus on the hearth.

OPPOSITE, TOP: Bell House. Master bedroom.

OPPOSITE, BOTTOM: Bell House. Entrance hall inglenook.

By the mid-1880s, a more formal (and explicitly historical) Colonial Revival idiom based on eighteenth-century sources materialized in the work of McKim, Mead & White. Although they continued for several years to utilize the modernized shingled colonial idiom, the new historicism—as exemplified in the Henry A. C. Taylor House (1883–85) and the Commodore William Edgar House (1884–86), both in Newport—had more evocative connections. Instead of the semi-medieval seventeenth-century origins of the Bell House, this more formal historicism drew very explicitly from the more classical eighteenth-century architecture that came to be labeled "Georgian." The Taylor House, destroyed in the 1950s, was originally envisioned in brick but changed to a clapboard exterior because of cost. Rigidly symmetrical with its large rectangular form and prominent central entrance, it recalled the Longfellow House. Large ribbed chimneys anchored the hipped roof with a balcony or widow's walk, and it was festooned with ornamental details—Federal- and Bulfinch-style porches, six Palladian windows on the first floor, and elaborate Adamesque swags. The interior contained a large central hall with an elliptical arch drawn from the Newport examples, and the library contained reproduction paneling derived from an old Newport room. The critic Sheldon described it as "very nearly a pure colonial."[33] The Taylor House's origins were clearly sophisticated, recalling the classic Georgian period, not the period of earlier settlement.[34]

An indication of this shift toward a more explicit historical recall were the actions of an AIA committee that investigated "the practice of American architects and builders during the colonial period and first fifty years of national independence." Serving on the committee were George Mason Jr. of Newport, Peabody and Longfellow of Boston, and Cleveland Cady and McKim of New York. Mason read the committee's report at the 1881 annual meeting. Tracing the growth of interest in the Colonial Revival style to the 1876 centennial celebration, the report noted the American tendency "to dream of an Arcadian existence and long to step back a hundred years into the past." However, the report added, while this may have been "poetical and delightful . . . we cannot be purists, we cannot bring ourselves back." Instead, the committee offered the following guidelines: "If not absolute copyists, we may however learn much from the past. . . . Let us therefore study the principles that shaped and guided the architecture of the colonial period and the first fifty years of American independence . . . [which] will reward us with an insight into the causes which led to the adoption of forms of construction which we now admire."

The committee suggested that rather than haphazardly applying details from a variety of sources, the architect should study the colonial past with more rigor.[35]

The Edgar House, a project on which McKim served as chief designer, carried further the new formality of colonial recall and also symbolized a quest for monumentalization.[36] Approached across a broad lawn with a circular drive, the main block of the house sat at the back of a low terrace of stone with a classical balustrade. Wings, pushed forward at either side, defined a forecourt. Hermetic in its removal from the street, the strict geometrical symmetry and gravitational balance of the exterior broke decisively with the shingled idiom. The overall form and the brick exterior may have derived from Virginia plantation houses, or perhaps from Philadelphia Georgian. However, the brownish-colored brick that was employed was Roman in size—perhaps the first usage in the United States—and not the more rectangular-shaped variety that had been used in the eighteenth century. Mortar was now white, conforming to eighteenth-century practice. The massive arched chimneys recall those at Stratford Hall and also Independence Hall.[37] Yet McKim and partners did not create a copy; the contrasting octagonal and elliptical bays and the second-floor porch indicated a lingering modernized colonial attitude and the desire to create a modern house.

To contemporary observers, McKim, Mead & White were creating a new style. Commenting on the house for *Art Age* magazine, one critic noted that the design of the Edgar House rejected the "oddity and straining effect" of many Newport residences, and its colonial style gave a "simplicity and broadness . . . a fit picture for the historical frame of Old Newport."[38] The Edgar House and the Taylor House both announced a new Colonial Revival idiom that sought more formal and evocative grandeur than the past and was more academic in the study of sources.

The work of McKim, Mead & White, Peabody, and others illuminates the characteristic approaches that would be brought to Colonial Revival throughout the next century and beyond. On the one hand was a loose approximation of the past, as with the "modernized colonial," where details were grafted onto different forms, while on the other was the academic approach in which more specific recall was the aim. American architects and critics began to follow these directions in various regional variations as they sought a solution to the dilemma of America's lack of a national style.

The World's Columbian Exposition in Chicago in 1893 heralded the ascendancy of the various colonial styles as expressions of American identity. Announced as a celebration of the 400th anniversary of Christopher Columbus's discovery of the New World, the exposition proclaimed the United

McKim, Mead & White, William Edgar House, Newport, Rhode Island, 1884–86.

States's emergence on the world stage as a major industrial, commercial, political, and imperial power. Central to the notion of American triumphalism was the establishment of an American history. The "White City," also called the Court of Honor, where architects such as McKim, Peabody, and others designed white classical palaces, referenced a European Renaissance heritage and posited that an equivalent American Renaissance was underway. The New World was a Renaissance discovery, and the United States was a child of that Renaissance. After losing its way architecturally during the nineteenth century, the country had rediscovered its classical past. In a sense, the Court of Honor was presented as America's historical backdrop.

While the Court of Honor served as the stage for a civic American architecture, its domestic identity was revealed in the state pavilions. Here, the Colonial Revival style triumphed. The Massachusetts state building by Peabody & Stearns, a house that paid homage to the demolished Hancock House, was explained as an "enlarged and enriched version of the home of the bold signer of the Declaration of Independence." [39] The Pennsylvania building, designed by Thomas P. Lonsdale, borrowed its tower from Independence Hall, placing it above a base of red brick with white trim, which resulted in a house that looked like a large villa. New Jersey chose Washington's headquarters in Morristown as the basis of its building, while California's building, by the San Francisco architect A. Page Brown (an alumnus of the McKim, Mead & White office) with assistance from Bernard Maybeck, borrowed from the designs of several of California's missions. Idaho's commissioners had Kirkland Cutter produce a giant log cabin to represent their state's heritage. Connecticut erected a supposed replica of an eighteenth-century colonial mansion with giant columns.

Several Southern states declined to build pavilions; however, Louisiana constructed an imitation Creole-style raised cottage of the late-eighteenth century. The Virginia building by Edgerton Rogers drew on the Potomac River facade of Mount Vernon. One critic, in describing the building, sneered, "The state did not furnish a building architecturally the equal of those of some of the other commonwealths . . . [still] the historic interest attached to the house far more than compensated." In fact, the Virginia building proved to be one of the most popular exhibits. Kentucky, Delaware, and West Virginia erected buildings that were identified as Southern by some observers.[40] Many other state buildings utilized colonial-era architectural elements, and their interiors often contained antiques and reproductions.

The Colonial Revival buildings at the World's Columbian Exposition confirmed that the United States had discovered its architectural past, or at least parts of it. Energized by what Chicago represented, architecture critic Howard Crosby Butler penned an article noting that the Colonial Revival style offered variety and differences between New England and the South; the solution was obvious: "The Colonial should be our national style; it originated here, is distinctively American and may be easily adapted to all the requirement of American life."[41] Many themes could be found at the fair of 1893, but the evocation of Early American architecture as a symbol of American identity and a variety of models to imitate stood out.

COLUMNITUS GIGANTICUS, OR THE OLD SOUTHERN COLONIAL

After the American Revolution, the large columnar portico began to appear, showing up at Woodlands in Philadelphia (1787–89), and in Thomas Jefferson's designs for the Virginia State House in Richmond (1785–98), and his remodeling of Monticello (1796–1817) and the design for the University of Virginia (1814–26). With Jefferson, and other architects of government buildings — such as Benjamin Henry Latrobe (1764–1820), Robert Mills (1781–1855), and Dr. William Thornton (1759–1828) — the intent, at least partially, was to adopt elements of classical antiquity as legitimizing agents for the new American experiment. Part of the international neoclassical recovery of Greek and Roman architecture of the late eighteenth and early nineteenth centuries was the American love affair with giant columns, which grew in intensity as columnar porticos were placed on banks, stores, and houses of all sizes and configurations.

The association of Southern colonial architecture with large columnar porticos began in the 1890s, fed by the myth of the "Old South" as a land of romance and large plantations ruled by benevolent masters with happy slaves toiling the fields. It was one of the more bizarre interpretations of colonial-era architecture, commonly called the "Old Southern Colonial." The term meant, quite simply, large houses with huge two-story columnar porticos. During this period, it is important to note, the image of the South was changing, if not being wholly reinvented. Through the novels, stories, and historical studies of authors such as Thomas Nelson Page, many of whom mixed fact with fiction, a misty, dewy-eyed picture of Southern gentility was evoked. Historians such as William Archibald Dunning joined in rejecting slavery as the cause of the Civil War, and instead focused on state's rights and economic considerations. In this reinvented South, the Civil War was reinterpreted as a consequence of the commercial and industrial power barons of the North crushing the benevolent South's agrarian economy. The Old South had been a land of cavaliers, of culture, good manners, and a Christian civilization, all of which had disappeared in the North. In some interpretations, the "Negro" was better off under slavery than freedom. This reinterpretation coincided with the introduction of Jim Crow laws and the fading of the blood bath of the war into a romantic haze of statuary programs and soldiers' reunions. In this mythic re-creation, the Southern plantation house of the colonial period became closely associated with a large columnar portico, even though such a feature normally did not appear until well into the nineteenth century and frequently was more common in city houses such as those in Natchez, Mississippi, than houses out in the countryside.[42]

Several state buildings at the 1893 World's Columbian Exposition contained large columnar porticos. Kentucky's building had a large Greek Doric Revival portico and was identified as "Southern." Illustrating the problem of such a regional identification, the Connecticut building by Warren R. Briggs of Bridgeport also had a gigantic two-story central portico, while below it and stretching to either side were single-story porches. Descriptions of the house ranged from "a typical Connecticut residence of a hundred years ago" to a more honest assessment: "[It was] such a mansion as anyone could wish his grandfather had lived in before the Revolution, and could be certain that he had not."[43] Two years after the fair, a correspondent for *American Architecture,* commenting on a St. Louis house that featured a great two-story portico and "large columns," asserted that the house was "almost part and parcel of the southern colonial." The writer added: "[The house] savors more of the southern Colonial architecture than its sister style of the Northeastern States."[44]

Though the giant portico appeared in the architecture of both the North and the South during the nineteenth century, it was inescapably identified as Southern and dating to the colonial period. This view is apparent in the article "Colonial Architecture for American Homes," published in architect George Barber's magazine *American Homes* in Knoxville, Tennessee. The writer briefly reviewed early America and concluded that the only "distinctive" architecture appeared in the South, especially in Virginia. He claimed that the large plantation house was "well served to impress" and appropriate for "entertaining large numbers of friends with its broad hall and open galleries." Elaborating on the subject, he wrote: "The great two-story colossal columns supporting a gabled pediment, so common in the Southern type, was capable of the greatest variety of treatment." The article contained only one illustration, a photograph of Arlington, the house of Robert E. Lee. The text that accompanied that photograph stated that "the position which its owner occupies in the hearts of his countrymen" was in line with the house's public character and that it provided a model for imitation. The article failed to mention that the giant Doric portico of Arlington was added in 1818, long after the colonial period, and that Lee was merely a later owner.[45]

The association of Southern colonial-era architecture with giant columns continued well into the 1950s, as is demonstrated by the comments of Thomas Mott Shaw, one of the restoration architects for Colonial Williamsburg: "To a Southerner, colonial means columns—and of course here at Williamsburg there were practically no columns. I think that Jefferson was very disappointed in the College of William and Mary because it didn't have any columns."[46] Here Shaw reveals a common perception of Southern Colonial architecture and the critical role played by Jefferson's postcolonial, or early Republic, designs and his employment of large porticos and columns—architectural features that later generations would call *colonial*.

The architecture of Curran R. Ellis of Macon, Georgia, effectively illustrates the colonial connections to the giant column. Macon, a city located in central Georgia on the Ocmulgee River, was a major trading port before the Civil War and later it recovered to become a railroad and manufacturing town. It was already known for its large antebellum homes, and its newly wealthy classes of the late nineteenth and early twentieth century were determined to outdo the past. They accomplished this through the work of several local architects, most notably Ellis, who gave them a regional architectural idiom.

Curran R. Ellis was born in Macon in 1872 into a locally prominent family. He graduated from Mercer University at the age of seventeen, apprenticed with a local architect, and then worked in Atlanta with the prominent firm of D. B. Denny. He returned to Macon in the late 1890s and quickly became the leading architect in the area (eventually he had several hundred buildings to his credit) and a political leader. His connections were legendary; one architect later recalled that when faced with competition for a court house, Ellis "bustled into the commissioners meeting room several minutes after the deadline had expired, apologized to the commissioners for being late, and placed his drawings up beside the coded entries. He got the job."[47]

Connecticut Building, World's Columbian Exposition, Chicago, Illinois, 1893.

Kentucky Building, World's Columbian Exposition, Chicago, Illinois, 1893.

CONNECTICUT STATE BUILDING.

KENTUCKY STATE BUILDING.

Curran R. Ellis, B. F. Adams House, Macon, Georgia, 1906 (remodeling and additions to house originally built 1842).

TOP: Adams House. View from hall to front parlor.

BOTTOM: Adams House. Rear parlor.

TOP: Adams House. Front parlor.

BOTTOM: Adams House. Bedroom.

Ellis designed numerous houses in the 1890s and 1900s that employed the colossal portico. Ten of his large-porticoed houses in Macon and Monticello, Georgia, and Eufaula, Alabama, received a write-up in the Atlanta-based *Southern Architect and Building News* under the title "Types of Colonial Homes." The article noted Ellis's reputation as a designer of "colonial residences," adding that he "has studied the colonial type of architecture devotedly." The article identified such large columnar houses as dating to before the Civil War, noting that, "On account of our climate and the temperament of our people, it has always been popular in the South, and that the Southerner still clings to it is but natural."[48] The truth was something altogether different, but to many Americans,

anything that smacked of antiquity evoked the colonial period.

Some of Ellis's work enhanced the earlier Greek Revival style, as in the case of a remodeling he carried out around 1906 for B. F. Adams, a cotton factor on College Avenue, which was one of the highest points in Macon. Adams had purchased a large 1842 house with six Doric columns. Ellis enlarged the house, adding several rooms to the rear, a porte-cochere to the side, and extended the porch around both sides, adding twelve columns to make a total of eighteen. Ellis also enlarged the front entrance and added a second-floor balcony. Inside, he kept the original central hall but extended the windows in the rooms on either side to floor

Curran R. Ellis, Eugene Harris House, Macon, Georgia, 1902.

OPPOSITE: Adams House. Portico.

level. Oak and walnut parquet flooring was installed along with up-to-date tile fireplace inserts. The expansion changed the house's features significantly, giving it a Parthenon-like appearance.

Ellis played the colossal-portico card in different ways, as exemplified by the Eugene Harris House of 1902, located a few hundred yards down the hill from the Adams House, on Georgia Avenue. For this new house, which would be built over a spring and adjacent to the large 1855 Italianate Hays

House, Ellis needed to create a commanding presence, and he accomplished this with a portico of four giant columns in front of a deep porch. The order Ellis employed combined several sources: the column was a variation on the Roman Doric with a decorated band at the capital and a blank shaft, while the cornice contained elements of the Corinthian order. The source books that Ellis looked to are unknown, but details in his work resemble plates found in Asher Benjamin's manuals of the first half of the nineteenth century.[49]

Ellis's training and background as a late-Victorian designer is evident in the excessive detail in his work. The entrance door has elaborately scaled-down elements. To each side are ornate window bays. The impressive interior hall with its

great staircase climbing up one side, the elaborate stained-glass windows of the opalescent variety, and the framed door openings have nothing to do with the Colonial Revival, the Federal style, or the Greek and Roman revivals. The Harris House, as with Ellis's other great houses, was pure American Gilded Age but sold as "Southern Colonial." *The Southern Architect* predicted that Ellis's work would be of interest to architects "everywhere" and "should serve as a stimulus to those who are making a closer style of the colonial."[50] The Old Southern Colonial became a national image with variations built across the country.

One of the Deep South's most prominent examples of *columnitus giganticus* is the McFaddin–Ward House (1906) in

OPPOSITE: Harris House. Entrance hall.

LEFT: Harris House. Detail of entrance.

RIGHT: Harris House. Front parlor.

OVERLEAF: Henry Conrad Mauer, McFaddin-Ward House, Beaumont, Texas, 1906.

Beaumont, Texas. The owners, the McFaddins, were a family with extensive land holdings, on whose property the great strike at Spindletop in 1901 touched off the beginnings of the Texas oil boom.[51] A McFaddin daughter, Di, and her husband, W. C. Averill, originally commissioned the house but shortly after completion they sold it to her brother and sister-in-law, W. P. H. (Perry) and Ida Caldwell McFaddin. The house then passed to their daughter Mamie Louise McFaddin, who married Carroll E. Ward. The Wards maintained the house and increased the collections. Mamie founded the Beaumont Heritage Society, which preserves the house to this day.

The architect of the McFaddin–Ward House was Henry Conrad Mauer , who was born in LaGrange, Texas, in 1873. Trained at the Pratt Institute in the Beaux Arts method, Mauer arrived in Beaumont in 1901, along with others attracted by the Lucas gusher, and set about transforming the town with a new sense of Eastern and Old Southern elegance. Throughout the next thirty-eight years, Mauer appropriated the giant portico for a number of residential projects in Beaumont and designed many civic and commercial buildings in the area.

McFaddin-Ward House. Entrance facade.

For the McFaddin-Ward design, Mauer essentially adopted the Connecticut building from the World's Columbian Exposition of 1893. He employed four giant Ionic columns to support a two-story-tall portico, and then underneath and around the sides he placed a single-story porch with twenty Ionic columns. Classical balustrades at four levels—including a widow's walk—vied for attention along with a small pediment on the entrance salient. As with Ellis's work in Macon, Mauer created a fictionalized version of the past. One article described it as "Southern Colonial" and "strictly Colonial with the Ionic order."[52] At 12,800 square feet, the McFaddin-Ward House reached mansion proportions on the order of Newport's "cottages" of those years, and while the central hall owed a debt to the living halls of McKim, Mead & White's shingled modernized colonial mode, it was now formalized with a grand staircase on axis. Although the house on current display reflects elements of Mamie Louise McFaddin-Ward's taste—as in the lighter-toned decorative treatment of the library rather than the original dark Arts and Crafts

ABOVE: McFaddin-Ward House. Library.

BELOW, LEFT: McFaddin-Ward House. Plan.

BELOW, RIGHT: McFaddin-Ward House. Entrance hall fireplace.

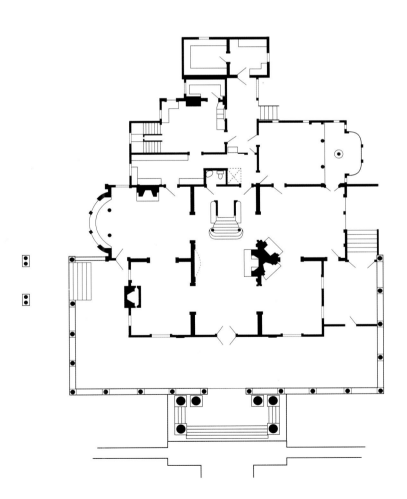

McFaddin-Ward House. Entrance hall.

treatment—much of the interior reflects the eclectic tastes of the period with Art Nouveau–styled glass, Rococo and William and Mary Revival furniture, and many other idioms. By the standards of the twenty-first century, the aesthetic is not Colonial Revival, but more in line with the tastes of the early twentieth century.

The giant porticos satisfied the Southerner's desires for both monumentality and neighborliness. The stately portico signaled that a person of importance resided there, while a porch acknowledged that the homeowner was "folks," an ordinary individual who could relax comfortably in full view, rocking and greeting his neighbors. But the giant portico also had its critics: Joseph Everett Chandler, a proper Boston Colonial Revivalist and restorer of colonial architecture, published a picture of a large-porticoed house with the caption "PURE 'HOPPIGEE COLONIAL' An example of everything not to do." Chandler claimed that this "Kickapoo" style came from faulty scholarship and his book was an attempt to separate true colonial from the "Virulent Colonial."[53]

PURE "HOPPIGEE COLONIAL."
An example of everything not to do.

ABOVE: "PURE 'HOPPIGEE COLONIAL' An example of everything not to do." Illustration in Joseph Everett Chandler's *The Colonial House* (1916).

BELOW: McFaddin-Ward House. Dining room.

A YANKEE MOUNT VERNON: HILL-STEAD, FARMINGTON, CONNECTICUT

Described by one scholar as "perhaps the finest Colonial Revival house," Hill-Stead represents a unique collaboration of Theodate Pope Riddle and the firm of McKim, Mead & White. Commanding a hilltop and gleaming white in a seemingly rural country setting, Hill-Stead evokes Washington's Mount Vernon fused with the rambling additive composition of New England saltboxes, blown-up to the scale of a grand country house. The novelist Henry James, who visited the house, described it as "the momentary effect of a magnified Mount Vernon." Filled with "modern 'impressionistic' pictures," Hill-Stead gave one "the momentary effect of a large slippery sweet inserted, without a warning, between the compressed lips."[54]

Theodate Pope, who married the diplomat John Wallace Riddle in 1916, can be described as a free-spirited wealthy woman who followed her inclinations and defied many of society's prescriptions. In addition to art and architecture, she was interested in psychic research, socialism, and educational reform. Born in 1867 in Cleveland to Alfred Atmore

and Ada Brooks Pope, Theodate grew up in prosperous surroundings. In addition to a house on Euclid "Millionaires Row" Avenue in Cleveland, the Popes had a New York apartment and traveled extensively. Alfred developed a passionate interest in art, but instead of collecting the typical old masters and safe salon paintings, he acquired major works by Whistler, Degas, Monet, Cassatt, and others, and had a large collection of Japanese prints. Theodate, very much her father's daughter, enjoyed a sense of freedom that was unusual for the period. Between 1886 and 1888, she attended Miss Porter's School in Farmington, Connecticut, and fell in love with the small New England town. After at least one unsuccessful courtship, Theodate convinced her parents to allow her to move back to Farmington, and in 1890 she commenced remodeling an older house in town. She had been attracted to architecture previously, and the experience with the remodeling project inspired her to try taking on something larger, such as a retirement house for her parents and a showcase for their art collection.

At the turn of the century, architecture as a profession was a rarity for women, with only a few such as Julia Morgan and Marion Mahoney succeeding. Pope never considered studying at an architecture school; instead she pursued an informal tutorial course in the history of art and architecture with a Princeton University professor and quickly began working on

Theodate Pope Riddle and McKim, Mead & White, Hill-Stead, Farmington, Connecticut, 1898–1901, 1906–7. South facade.

ABOVE: Hill-Stead.

OVERLEAF: Hill-Stead. West facade.

plans. With her father's money, Pope purchased some small farms adjacent to Farmington and determined the site of the house with the aid of the Boston landscape architect Warren Manning. Then she set out to secure an architect. McKim, Mead & White were the preeminent firm, and she approached them since they were deeply involved with John Howard Whittemore and his family in nearby Naugatuck. Pope wrote to Mead in June 1898, just before embarking on a European trip, requesting plans of "a beautifully planned house in thoroughly good style and self-contained and dignified." She did not want an elevation drawing, explaining that "what time you have spent on this preliminary plan have the man spend in thought and not in lines with fancy lead coloring. We know all that." The job became more complicated when, in September, her father suggested she submit her own plans to McKim, Mead & White. She then wrote to Mead again: "I am writing for and in the interests of my father. We have now decided instead of having you submit sketches to us, to send you the plans that I have been working over at

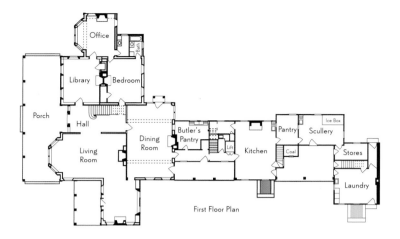

ABOVE: Hill-Stead. Plan.

BELOW: Hill-Stead. Living room.

OPPOSITE: Hill-Stead. View from hall to living room.

Hill-Stead. Bedroom.

intervals for some years to draw to scale and make an elevation of in the event of our coming to a mutual agreement. Consequently, as it is my plan, I expect to decide in all the details as well as all more important questions of plan that may arise. This must be clearly understood at the outset, so as to save unnecessary friction in the future. In other words, it will be a Pope house instead of a McKim, Mead and White." In conclusion, she wrote: "I will say that I am not nearly as difficult to deal with as this would seem, for I am very tolerant of advice and always open to suggestions and good reasoning."[55]

Why Mead ever agreed to such a proposition remains unclear. Perhaps he did not wish to alienate the Whittemores, for whom several large buildings were under way. Perhaps Mead believed the job would revert to the firm once the client's plans proved to be wanting. Pope's original drawings do not survive but all the evidence indicates that the McKim, Mead & White draftsman put in charge of the project, Edgerton Swartwout, followed her directives in terms of room arrangement and style of the house. By late September 1898,

Pope had the site surveyed and drew a footprint of the house. Swartwout met several times with Pope, and she barraged the McKim, Mead & White office with drawings, corrections, and her ideas. The barns received special attention along with roof pitches. As she explained: "[I] Have intentionally drawn these roofs at different pitches." She insisted upon different clapboard widths for the barn, and she wanted a dovecote. In February 1899, Swartwout produced a set of drawings that, among other things, depicted a large boxy main house with a long service wing and a stable and barns to the rear—all in keeping with the footprint that Pope gave them.[56]

However, Pope mandated more changes and supervised construction of the house, hiring a local builder from Unionville, Richard F. Jones, and local master-carpenter Hal Mason. Under her direction, a bay window was inserted in the front elevation; then, the south elevation and carriage entrance were subjected to her scrutiny. She proceeded to create an informal summer dining room and an extended porte cochere. The biggest change, however, came in October 1901, after the Popes had, at least partially, taken residence in the house. Pope recorded in her diary that Mead had

Hill-Stead. Bedroom.

arrived and helped with "suggestions about the porch we are going to put across the front of the house." In March, Pope had traveled in Virginia and took pictures of Mount Vernon. Between 1906 and 1907, a small office was added to the north end of the west front, and the library was extended into the original office. McKim, Mead & White and their lead draftsman F. J. Adams largely handled this addition, just as they did the rebuilding of the barn after a fire in the spring of 1908, though in doing so they followed Pope's original scheme. Moreover, most of the interior details appear to be the product of Pope. The great hall with its arch recalls Carter's Grove in Virginia, a house she could have seen during her trip there, if she hadn't already seen depictions of it in several of the architecture books that she owned.[57]

Why Pope was somewhat uninvolved in Hill-Stead's 1906–7 extension can be attributed to her having been distracted by her work involving the design and construction of Westover School (1903–9) in Middlebury, Connecticut. Intensely interested in educational reform, she followed this particular project using the design of the Hop Brook School in Naugatuck. In 1913, before going on to design several buildings, including, most prominently, Avon Old Farms School (1915–27) in Avon, Connecticut, Pope opened an office in New York.

The west front of Hill-Stead recalls Mount Vernon's portico; however, it is Mount Vernon with the Chinese Chippendale railings that had been installed after Washington's death (the railings were later removed in a restoration campaign of the twentieth century). To this facade, Pope added bay windows and wings. The south facade, which contains the porte cochere (the usual means of access to the house), resembles a long and large strung-out New England saltbox. The clapboards on the main house are all of an even width, and the nail heads create a pattern. The shutters are dark green, in keeping with the New England custom that developed in the nineteenth century. The attached stable/barn complex is more decidedly rustic.

Inside the house, the main public rooms of the front section, characterized by a central hall and stairs with rooms to either side, can be interpreted as having been inspired by

Frederick Thomas Harris, William F. Holt House, Redlands, California, 1903.
East facade.

eighteenth-century houses. But the scale is much expanded and the generous flow of space from the hall into the living room, with its large windows and bays (designed specifically for Alfred Pope's large girth), indicate a very different sensibility at work.[58] Woodwork and trim throughout the interior are indicative of Pope's—and McKim, Mead & White's—employment of eighteenth-century pattern books, but these features are kept appropriately simple. Wall coverings are classical in inspiration but not copies of colonial-period patterns. For the interior, the focus was on the amazing collection of art: a Degas pastel, *The Jockeys,* hangs over the fireplace in the dining room; a row of Whistler prints lines the wall that guides the stairs; a Monet, *Haystack,* and a Manet dominate the living room; Whistler's *Blue Wave* fits into the space above the mantel in the library addition.

The acreage of Hill-Stead stood at about 250, and neatly stacked stone walls subdivided it into different sections. Alfred Pope got a six-hole golf course in the meadow below the house. A kitchen garden was tucked into the rear of the service wing, and a large sunken garden occupied a natural declivity south of the main entry. Warren Manning and Theodate Pope designed the sunken garden in a geometrical pattern, though in 1916 Beatrix Jones Farrand supplied a planting plan. The grounds of the estate also had several eighteenth-century structures, including a farmhouse and barn, which were later enlarged before being made into a model farm, complete with a Guernsey herd. Tranquil and evocative of both Virginia and New England, Hill-Stead received extensive publicity and caused Henry James to search for a metaphor when pressed to describe the place, saying that it "made everything else shrivel and fade: it was like the sudden trill of a nightingale, lord of the hushed evening."[59]

MISSION REVIVAL: HOLT HOUSE, REDLANDS, CALIFORNIA

The William F. Holt House illuminates the West's search for a regional colonial identity against the dominance of the East Coast and English-inspired imagery. Designed by Frederick T. Harris in 1903, the Holt House looks back to the Spanish settlement and the chain of missions erected up the coast of Alta California, from San Diego to Solano, between 1769 and 1823. Mexico's independence from Spain left many missions dormant, and during the next fifty years many of these structures were badly mutilated or destroyed. Beginning in the 1870s and 1880s and contemporary with the East Coast's

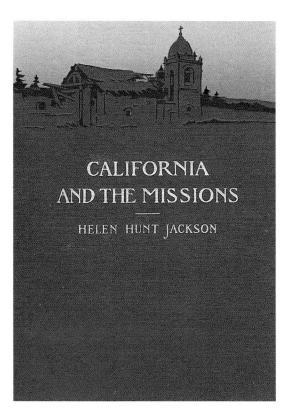

Cover of Helen Hunt Jackson's *California and the Missions* (1883).

development of the Colonial Revival, some East Coast transplants began to view the missions in a romantic light. Through the writings of Helen Hunt Jackson, especially works such as *California and the Missions* (1883), with its evocative illustrations, and her aforementioned bestselling novel of 1884, *Ramona,* the crumbling bell towers, ruined sun-struck adobe walls, shady arcades, and red-tile roofs acquired a poignancy that was very appealing to East Coast transplants. By 1888, Charles Fletcher Lummis, a Harvard-educated writer, had founded the Association for the Preservation of the Missions (it was renamed the Landmarks Club in 1895). Confirming the state's identification with Mission architecture was the Mission-styled California building at the World's Columbian Exposition. Following its unveiling there, the Mission Revival took off in California and, to a lesser degree, in other states, with hotels in major tourist destinations being designed in the idiom, examples of which include the Mission Inn in Riverside, California, and railroad stations across the state. The designer Gustav Stickley, a leader of the Arts and Crafts movement in the United States, praised the missions: "What would have been the result if the Franciscans of Spanish California and the Puritans of Plymouth Rock had exchanged continent-sides on coming to America? For one thing we should have missed the most superb and harmonious type of architecture known to the new continent—the architecture of the Old Missions."[60] Despite the ironies of Mission Revival (the original buildings were constructed by Spanish padres attempting to convert Indians to Catholicism) and the fact that those who built Mission-styled houses and buildings were, in most cases, resolutely Protestant and usually suspicious of anything Catholic, the romance of history overcame the prejudices and Mission Revival eventually surfaced in Protestant churches and many other building types.

The city of Redlands was founded in the late 1870s as a citrus center. Situated about sixty miles east of Los Angeles, it was "discovered" in the late 1880s as a winter resort by the Smiley Brothers, who were already owners of Mohonk House, New Paltz, New York. The Smileys, seeking a warm-weathered winter resort destination, indulged in some land development in Redlands, eventually constructing several buildings in the city, including the Mission-Romanesque

Holt House. Porch.

A. K. Smiley Library (1897). They succeeded in luring wealthy Easterners and others to build large houses and, in some cases, estates among the orange groves and along the town's wide streets.[61]

William F. and May Holt were among this wealthy group; their fourteen room, 5,600-square-foot house had a bowling alley in the basement and occupied two lots on the corner of Olive and Alvarado streets. The building permit they filed on July 11, 1903, estimated the cost at $19,000. Holt made his money developing the Imperial Valley in Southern California. Beginning in 1900, he purchased and sold land in the fertile valley, bringing in water for irrigation and founding the towns of El Centro, Brawley, and Holtville. Known as "the father of the Imperial Valley," Holt memorably appears as the banker of virtue and honest enterprise, Jefferson Worth, in the novel *The Winning of Barbara Worth* (1911). Frequent meetings under Spanish-styled arcades are a feature of the novel, which was one of the first million-copy bestsellers. The book's author, Harold Bell Wright, served as a minister in Redlands from 1907 to 1909, was a close friend of the Holts, and lived for a period in the caretaker's quarters in the house's stable. In 1926, the novel became a hit movie, introducing Gary Cooper to the screen.[62]

The house's architect, Frederick Thomas Harris, was born in 1866 in nearby San Bernardino. In 1902, Harris moved to Redlands to take advantage of the influx of wealth. His architecture displays an awareness of East Coast idioms and ideas. He remained in Redlands until 1913, when he moved south to El Centro, where he continued to work for Holt. Harris died

Holt House. North facade.

Holt House. Entrance hall.

in San Bernardino in 1922. His son, Harwell Hamilton Harris, born in Redlands in 1903, had a notable career as a modern-era architect, developing a regional Southern California idiom in the 1930s through the 1950s.[63]

The Holt House exemplifies the Mission Revival style with its broad, rounded single-story arches, scalloped parapet for the porch and porte cochere, dramatic Baroque front gable and smaller curved gables, adobe-colored stucco walls, low tower, red tile roofs, and round-headed windows. Most of the original California missions were abstemious with ornament, but the Holt House glories in a combination of Spanish, Romanesque, and Moorish plaques, rosettes, moldings, and square columns. The looping arcade, lifted off the ground by a high basement, and the deep shadows and excited skyline give the house an animated effect.

The ground floor is organized around a series of interconnected rooms with wide doorways, which, due to generous windows, provide a feeling of free-flowing space. The house has two entrances: the front door and two-story hall; and the porte cochere to the side with its own hall. The interior detailing includes hosts of engaged columns at every door, above which are pediments adorned with Adamesque wreaths—a design that is more East Coast Colonial Revival than Mission. The dining room contains a large built-in sideboard.

A landmark of the Mission Revival, the Holt House illuminates the broad regionalism of the Colonial Revival impulse. Popular for about twenty years, Mission Revival houses and buildings were constructed throughout the Southwest and elsewhere. However, to some critics they

Holt House. Entrance hall inglenook.

lacked sophistication, and in the 1910s a more historical Spanish Colonial Revival supplanted them.

HAMILTON HOUSE: "HALF WHIMSICAL, HALF LOVING SYMPATHY"

In 1881, Sarah Orne Jewett described the Hamilton House in South Berwick, Maine, as "unrivaled for the beauty of its situation, and for a certain grand air which I have found it hard to match in any house I have ever seen." In 1899, Jewett convinced the wealthy Bostonian Mrs. George Tyson and her stepdaughter, Elizabeth Tyson, to purchase the house and its 110 acres. Two years later, Jewett's novel *The Tory Lover* (1901) opens with: "The last day of October in 1777, Colonel Jonathan Hamilton came out of his high house on the river bank." In the book, the house, its "great room" and "stately dining room" in particular, serves as a stage set for meetings, dinners, and romantic interludes. At one such dinner, the

character John Paul Jones observes: "You live like a Virginia gentleman, sir, here in your Northern home." The only problem with Jewett's portrayal was that the construction of the Hamilton House came about four years after the Treaty of Paris of 1783, and consequently the house never contained the scenes she set therein.[64]

Built around 1787 for Colonel Jonathan Hamilton, the house was the center of his shipping and shipbuilding empire. Located on a bluff overlooking the Salmon Falls River, which flowed into the Piscataqua River and the Atlantic Ocean, his wharfs and warehouses were engaged in international trade of timber, rum, molasses, and slaves. When the river silted up and the economy changed to manufacturing, the house became a tenement for workers in a brick factory. However, the area around the Piscataqua was soon discovered as a summer retreat for the wealthy. Jewett, assuming the house would be lost to the area's new development, embarked on a campaign to save

Herbert W. C. Browne, Hamilton House, South Berwick, Maine, 1787, with additions 1899 onward. Photograph ca. 1920 by Elsie Tyson Vaughn.

the house, ultimately convincing the Tysons to purchase it. Mrs. George Tyson (Emily) was the widow of the late president of the Baltimore and Ohio Railroad. Her stepdaughter Elizabeth, also known as Elise, later married Henry G. Vaughn.

The decrepit house needed attention. The Tyson's hired Boston architect Herbert W. C. Browne to oversee its restoration and enhancement. Browne, a member of the "colonial trinity," which also included Ogden Codman Jr. and Arthur Little, was born in 1860 and grew up in the stately Peter Banner–designed Crafts House (1805), located in the Roxbury section of Boston. After studies in Paris and Florence and time in a Boston architect's office, Browne joined Little around 1890 to form what became a very successful partnership. Little & Browne designed city and country places, usually in the Colonial-Georgian idiom, for the Boston elite. Their best-known work was the large English Georgian Lars Anderson House in Washington, D.C.—now the headquarters of the Society of the Cincinnati.[65]

Browne, along with colleague Lester Couch, began work on the Hamilton House in 1899 and returned many times to make alterations and offer advice. Although Browne did most

Hamilton House. East facade and garden.

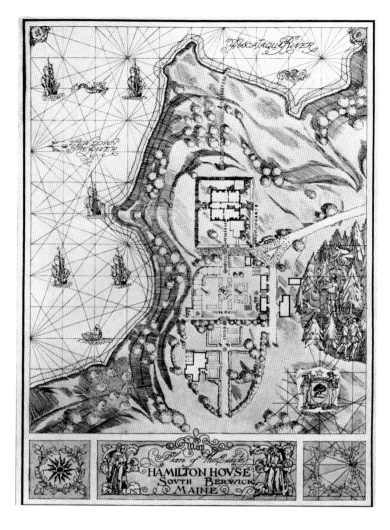

of the design, the Tysons were ultimately in charge and thus must be given equal credit for the house, the garden, and the garden cottage. Mrs. Tyson died in 1922, but thereafter Elise continued to make alterations. An amateur photographer of considerable talent, she documented the changing nature of the house over the years. Persuaded by architect William Sumner Appleton not to sell the house but to leave it to the Society for the Preservation of New England Antiquities (SPNEA), Elsie Vaughn died in 1949. Initially, SPNEA tried to return the house to its eighteenth-century appearance, removing some of the Tyson-Browne additions. However, in recent years they have begun to restore some of the house's Colonial Revival elements.

Respecting the classic proportions of the nearly square house, Brown and the Tysons determined to keep the modern improvements nonintrusive. Hence, to the north side two small wings were added that housed, on the northwest and toward the river, a porch, and on the northeast or garden side, a kitchen and china pantry. Encased in lattice and Chinese Chippendale railings, the wings were covered by vines, which provided camouflage and linked the house to the landscape. The doorways were enhanced to allow the passage of more light, some windows were lengthened, and, for the first time, shutters were added to the house. In contrast to typical architectural elaborations, the roof's original balustrade was not restored.

Inside, a back stair hall was removed from the dining room to provide more space, and bathrooms were installed. The major change involved the wall covering in several of the rooms. Initially, the wallpapers were fashionable floral patterns, typical of summer homes of the 1890s. The interior furnishings were similarly standard: wicker, a few antiques, and some painted chairs. Interest in historical wallpapers grew with the publication of Kate Sanborn's *Old Time Wall Papers: An Account of Pictorial Papers on Our Forefathers' Walls* (1905). By 1899, the Tysons and Browne had already installed in the hallway a replica of Jonathan Hamilton's original 1780s wallpaper, a series of superimposed Renaissance arches and columns with urns and swags. They commissioned this from the Boston firm of Gregory & Brown. The interest in classicizing the interior probably came through the recently published *Decoration of Houses* by Wharton and Codman, who, while dismissing wallpapers, argued for treating walls in an architectural manner. By 1905, the Tysons had wintered in Italy and had become aware that wall painting, or fresco painting, was,

TOP: Hamilton House. Main floor and garden plan.

BOTTOM: Hamilton House. Garden and cottage.

in the words of Wharton and Codman, one of the "noblest forms of wall-decoration." Another probable influence was Wharton's *Italian Villas and Their Gardens* (1904), which contained illustrations by Maxfield Parrish along with Wharton's assertion that elements of Italian gardens could work in America.[66] The Tysons hired George Porter Fernald, a Boston muralist, to paint Italian landscape and garden scenes in the dining room on top of the floral wallpaper they had installed a few years earlier. The scenes connected the room to the garden beyond.

Next, the Tysons, Browne, and Fernald focused on altering the parlor. On top of that room's floral wallpaper, Fernald painted a Seine-like Piscataqua River that flowed around the room with classical quays, balustrades, embankments, columns, and elegantly dressed ladies and gentlemen. Ships floated in the river, some off-loading furniture and china from foreign ports. Lining the bank stood Georgian- and Federal-style houses, a fort, and other structures. All of the buildings came from the vicinity, with one exception: in a corner (and sometimes concealed by an open door) Fernald placed a replica of Jefferson's Monticello. By implication, this small room was connected to the broader world of classical architecture, republican virtues, and international economy. America's colonial past stood as an equivalent to the Italian classical scenes shown in the dining room.

On the east side of the house, adjacent to the dining room with its Italian scenery, the Tysons and Browne cultivated what they thought was a garden in the style of the colonial period. The designer remains unclear, though muralist Fernald

Hamilton House. Detail of wall painting in parlor.

may have had some influence. Vine-covered pergolas surrounded a cross-axial plan containing four equal parts. Classical columns, urns, and other elements helped define the boundaries. Perennials of all types were planted in abundance. Statues of Greek goddesses and George and Martha Washington were added. The garden and the house soon became well known, and by 1909, articles appeared praising the work.[67]

Near the large garden, the Tysons created a small cottage garden and a structure that was described by one visitor as "a little house fit for a Hans Anderson story." It was constructed around 1907, possibly with the involvement of Browne. The Tysons had purchased some paneling and other elements from a house dating to around 1740 that was about to be demolished in a nearby town. The parts were creatively reused inside the garden cottage. Old framing members and joints were left exposed; a paneled fireplace wall was stripped of paint and became the major interior focal point. Above the fireplace, the former front door covered the chimney stack, and stair balusters were reused as small balconies. Old paneled doors and window shutters covered new cabinets on other walls. A few large arched studio windows permitted light and referenced the arch in the stair hall of the main house.

Hamilton House. Parlor.

Over a quarter of a century later, Elise Tyson Vaughn observed the changing attitudes toward the reuse of these fragments when she wrote: "In these days of more careful correctness in detail, especially in early American affairs, it, probably, would have been planned differently. But that was the year 1907 before the early American had fully come into his kingdom!"[68]

OGDEN CODMAN JR. AND THE CLASSICIZING OF THE COLONIAL

As one-third of the "colonial trinity," Ogden Codman became known and respected for his research on colonial-period architecture. Codman was born in 1863 in Boston, and his family owned a large colonial/Federal-era house, The Grange, located in Lincoln, Massachusetts, where he spent portions of his youth. His uncle, John Hubbard Sturgis, the Boston architect, had measured the John Hancock House prior to its demolition in 1863. Years later, Codman explained to fellow architect Fiske Kimball that his grandparents, "desiring to encourage my interest in old buildings," took him to see various works by Bulfinch and other early buildings in Boston "[which] had a charm and dignity unequaled . . . restrained and simple." Codman's real research and recording of colonial treasures began in the mid 1880s, when, after living in France with his parents and an unsatisfactory year at the architecture school at the Massachusetts Institute of Technology, he began knocking on the doors of various architects' offices in Lowell and Boston and became acquainted with Little & Browne. His interest lay with the more classical, or Georgian, models, for as he told William Sumner Appleton: "Those early houses were not architectural enough . . . I want a sort of artistic interest in the design of the house. . . . And even then it must be a bit classic."[69]

Codman's initial success came when Edith and Teddy Wharton hired him to design the interiors of their Newport house, Land's End. Edith Wharton later listed Codman with Charles McKim and Stanford White as "men of exceptional intelligence" who "had at last stirred the stagnant air of old New York." Much of Codman's work followed French and English precedent, for as he and Edith Wharton argued in *The Decoration of Houses* (1897), the basis of all good design and taste lay with following the classical models which originated with the Renaissance and continued with seventeenth- and eighteenth-century styles such as Georgian. A "general decline of taste which marked the middle of the present [nineteenth] century" was being reversed in the United States by the recovery of classicism and Georgian architecture. This movement advocated a type of scientific eclecticism,

or the close study of very specific models and their replication. Codman produced several studies of ideal colonial-era houses that could be classified as severely classical with their applied orders and appropriately subservient wings.[70]

Berkeley Villa, also known as Bellevue House, the mansion Codman designed in 1910 for his cousin Martha Codman near the head of Bellevue Avenue in Newport, Rhode Island, stands as his summary of the colonial house and its classical basis. Years later, Codman shared with Kimball his thoughts about Newport: "I did not think much of the collection of architectural types our multi-millionaires assembled there, utterly neglecting to follow the example set them in colonial times." Approached across a forecourt, the brick and wood gates, posts, and pineapple finials were based on the Nathaniel Heyward House in Charleston, South Carolina. The entrance facade was severely formal, inspired by the designs of several houses he had visited and photographed or measured. The story heights, roofline, and dormers were borrowed from the Shirley–Eustis house in Roxbury, Massachusetts, that had been attributed to Newport colonial architect Peter Harrison. For the double columns at the center and the projecting vestibule, Codman looked to the Eben Crafts House, also known as Elmwood, another Roxbury house, designed about 1805 by Peter Banner. For the south, or garden elevation, Codman took an octagonal bay and second-story loggia from Charles Bulfinch's Perez Morton House (1796), also located in Roxbury.[71]

If a certain New England restraint typified the exterior, especially when contrasted with other Newport "cottages," the interior of Berkeley Villa created a spatial drama. One enters on axis into a cylindrical stair hall and then turns on a cross axis to the drawing room and a view of the garden located on the south side. Codman pushed the house to the north side of the site to give room for a walled formal garden and terrace to the south, and also to shield the occupants from the noise of the hotel that stood next door. The stair hall appears to have been drawn from a scheme by James Paine, published in his 1767 book *Plans, Elevations, and Sections of Noblemen's and Gentlemen's Houses.* Although Codman admitted the English source, he claimed an American-French origin as well, in addition to citing the circular stair hall of the New York City Hall by Joseph Mangin and James McComb that had been built between 1802 and 1811. The French sophistication of New York's City Hall appealed to many

OPPOSITE: Fiske Kimball, tea/garden house, Berkeley Villa, Newport, Rhode Island, 1926.

OVERLEAF: Ogden Codman Jr., Berkeley Villa, Newport, Rhode Island, 1910.

TOP: Berkeley Villa. Bedroom.

BOTTOM: Berkeley Villa. Sitting room.

TOP: Berkeley Villa. Sitting room.

BOTTOM: Berkeley Villa. Bedroom.

architects of the period, including McKim in the 1870s. With his cousin at his side, Codman shopped in London for furniture and other decorative items before convincing her to give the interior work to the firm of Lenygon & Morant, who were located at 31 Old Burlington Street. They supplied some of the furniture, which was in appropriate Chippendale and other eighteenth-century styles, and the cornice moldings, door trims, and other decorative items. Writing from London to one of his office men, Codman offered advice about handling his cousin: "Miss Codman is thinking of haveing [*sic*] the rooms pannelled [*sic*] in wood, do not discourage her, as it is much nicer and more correct, if somewhat more expensive." Some of the mantels were composites drawn from various English sources.[72]

The garden of Berkeley Villa followed a formal scheme—French in inspiration with a pond and clipped trees. Codman closed his New York office and moved to France in 1920. So, when his cousin contacted him and expressed a desire to add a teahouse for the garden, Codman recommended she contact Fiske Kimball. For design inspiration, Kimball looked to the teahouse that was designed and built by Samuel McIntire for Elias Hasket Derby's house at Salem, Massachusetts, in 1794. Kimball was already at work on his study of McIntire, though it would not be published for many years.[73] With great fidelity, Kimball duplicated McIntire's design, though he left off some carved statues on top of the roof. A fitting complement to Codman's house, Kimball's design foreshadowed the archaeological correctness that appeared with greater frequency in the next several decades when the Colonial Revival triumphed as the American national expression for houses.

ABOVE: Berkeley Villa. Detail of library.

BELOW: Berkeley Villa. First floor plan and longitudinal cross section.

OPPOSITE: Berkeley Villa. Entrance hall.

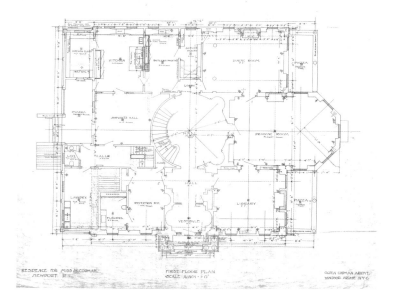

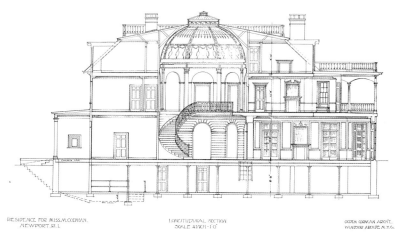

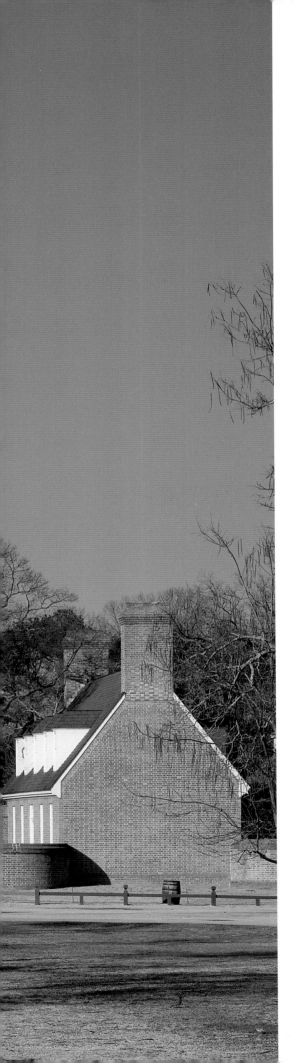

Triumph

THE 1910S TO WORLD WAR II

Between 1910 and 1940, the colonial aesthetic could be seen in the majority of America's houses, irrespective of household income. A prominent historian observed that the "most prolific source of inspiration in house design has been the Georgian and colonial of our own country's youth." A. Lawrence Kocher, a writer who surveyed the styles of country houses published in architectural magazines between 1922 and 1925, found the Colonial Revival style to be the absolute favorite, accounting for nearly fifty percent of all houses shown. Close behind were domestic architecture styles of sixteenth-, seventeenth-, and eighteenth-century England, which comprised about twenty percent, followed by the revival styles associated with Spain and France. In this work, Kocher proffered a lesson: "Good results have not come from the desire to be original or from the desire to disregard what has been done in the past." He concluded (with an aim at the nascent modernism lurking in the wings): "No architecture has been raised up suddenly out of newness to a notable era in creative art."[1]

Elements of the Colonial Revival style became the working idiom of the interior design and decoration trade, dominating the decorative arts and furniture markets. One writer of the period succinctly summarized the Colonial Revival style's dominance at the time: "The story of America is the story of colonial furniture."[2] Colonial-era imagery could be found in paintings, on the

Perry, Shaw & Hepburn, Governor's Palace, Colonial Williamsburg, Virginia, 1932–36.

stage, and in movies, and it provided the backdrop for many novels, including bestsellers by Kenneth Roberts and Walter D. Edmunds. Moreover, the Colonial Revival aesthetic became the image of choice for all types of buildings. The federal government adapted it for post offices and courthouses, as did the great WPA mural program of the 1930s. Colonial Williamsburg, which began in the late 1920s but did not open its first building until 1932, helped further popularize a selected view of the American past. Both a restoration and a new creation, Colonial Williamsburg, through its marketing of its house plans, colors, and furniture reproductions, became a prototype for living, one to which many Americans aspired. Perhaps the greatest tastemaker of twentieth-century America, Colonial Williamsburg was arguably the greatest American design of that century as well.

During this period, especially in academic circles, the Colonial Revival's dominance was being challenged by the growing strength of modernism. The various Colonial Revival styles, of course, were the antidote to the modern house. In 1923, one critic claimed that the modern style had little following in the United States. The critic described its "flat, angular, and dirty-colored surfaces" as "born of a restless and simian desire for novelty." But in the next decade, modern gained adherents, and by the mid-1930s, many of the architectural periodicals, the same ones that had published Colonial Revival designs, changed their loyalties. A war of words broke out, with traditionalists employing terms such as "Nudist Homes." The modernists counterattacked; Frank Lloyd Wright, speaking at the College of William and Mary, called the Williamsburg restoration a "hangover" that showed "a mawkish sentimentality for a past that wasn't any good." The response, which was rather chilling given the racial situation in Virginia, came a few days later in an article that urged that modern houses be "segregated" and claimed that "they clash with the Georgian; they destroy the illusion of the eighteenth century that is precious to most of us."[3]

Colonial Revival–style house design during these decades incorporated many interpretations of form, details, and sources, thus perpetuating the debate of the "modernized" Colonial Revival look versus the more "formal" and historically accurate expression. There were those architects who very freely—and loosely—adopted Colonial Revival motifs and details and applied them to forms that had little to do with the Early American past, such as a gambrel-roofed Sears, Roebuck and Company kit house, while other architects demanded great fidelity to original sources. Of course previously unknown buildings and details appeared continuously, resulting in everchanging interpretations.

PUBLICATIONS

Central to the triumph of the Colonial Revival style as the national image for the home was a giant publication effort that documented early America. Building on the earlier efforts of McKim's photographs, along with Barry and Little's books of sketches and drawings, new publications on the colonial past arrived like a tidal wave after 1910. The number of articles published is in the tens of thousands, and a count of books published on the subject in these years would easily be more than a thousand.[4] They may be categorized in several ways.

First were those publications that verged on the tourist guide, many of which often depicted colonial buildings and details as if viewed through a romantic haze. *New Hampshire Beautiful* (1923; 1935), an installment in Wallace Nutting's series on the states, as well as Samuel Chamberlin's photographs, in particular *Open House in New England* (1937), are among the many that popularized colonial-period architecture as the foundation stone of America and suitable for the present.

Although the East Coast dominated the architectural publishing industry, other regions garnered notice as well. California received the most attention from books, as exemplified by volumes such as Hannaford and Edward's *Spanish Colonial or Adobe Architecture of California, 1800–1850* (1931), and Rexford Newcomb's *The Spanish House for America* (1927). Newcomb, an architect and historian, produced a host of books on different areas, each blending history with an application for contemporary houses.[5] Midwestern locales received attention too, as seen in the work of I. T. Frary, who authored a book on Ohio's early architecture and advised on new buildings such as Malabar Farm.

"The Adams," from the Sears Roebuck Company *Book of Modern Homes* (1920).

Cover of Rexford Newcomb's *The Spanish House for America* (1927).

Many of the histories were written to spur appreciation and preservation of early buildings. Harold Eberlein, a prolific author, observed that he desired to aid in the "interpretation of modern buildings" and "supply a measure of inspiration and guidance to those who propose building homes for themselves."[6] His book, which was the first comprehensive book-length study on the subject, followed Schuyler's early lead in treating postcolonial and Greek Revival architecture as part of the larger colonial story.

The *White Pine Series of Architectural Monographs,* which appeared bimonthly between 1915 and 1940, illustrated the diverse intentions of some treatments of colonial-era architecture. Initially published and funded under the auspices of several American timber companies and their trade associations (with major support from Weyerhauser Forest Products), one of the primary purposes of the series was to provide accurate details that would be suitable for reproduction by architects and builders.[7] The need for prototypical details led to a search for the ignored or the unknown, or as Aymar Embury II, an architect and historian, observed in an early issue: "Long after the Colonial work of New England and the South became well known to the architects, and had become regarded by them as a suitable source from which to draw precedents for modern work, the remaining examples of the work of the Dutch in their colony of New Netherlands remained unnoticed and neglected." The *White Pine Series* published a tremendous range of building types, though the

primary focus remained houses. The volumes contained a minimal amount of text in addition to photographs and measured drawings of the featured buildings; their exquisite details gave the architect and builder a whole new repertory of forms and ornament that could be reproduced. In addition, many of the early issues unveiled new designs featuring colonial details and forms. The main editor of the series, Russell F. Whitehead, also produced a book of colonial styles for modern homes and claimed that new Colonial Revival houses were representative of "American ideals" and "American culture."[8]

Fiske Kimball's *Domestic Architecture of the American Colonies and Early Republic* (1922) ranks as the most important book on the history of American architecture to appear in these years. Although it is a history of the period 1600 to 1820, Kimball addresses the contemporary scene, noting the "revival [of colonial forms], after constant gains in knowledge and strength, [which] constitutes to-day perhaps the most powerful force in American domestic architecture." According to Kimball, the classicism inherent in the work was a "permanent national style." In his subsequent volume, *American Architecture* (1925), Kimball argued that classicism provided the basis for American architecture and asserted, "To us the Colonial style, with all its provincial charm, is still in leading strings."[9]

In opposition to Kimball's exaltation of the Colonial Revival were the naysayers, such as architecture critic Lewis Mumford. Inspired by Van Wyck Brooks's project for a "usable past," Mumford, writing in *Sticks and Stones* (1924), argued that "what we call a revival is really a second burial." His castigation cut deep: "What we have built in the colonial mode is all very well in its way: unfortunately, it bears the same relation to the work of the late-seventeenth and early-eighteenth centuries that the Woolworth Building bears to the cathedrals of the Middle Age." Actually, Mumford found some value in the early New England village, which he defined as a "common holding of the land by the community, and the cooperative ownership and direction of the community itself." This he interpreted as "a garden-city in every sense," and he admired the "Medieval tradition" and organic quality of the colonial-era house.[10] This view exemplified the ideology of the United States Regional Planning Association and its Green Belt communities, including that at Radburn, New Jersey, designed by Henry Wright and Clarence Stein.

Many guidebooks published during this period informed architects and interior designers how to build and furnish a Georgian-style, Federal-style, Dutch Colonial–style, or Spanish Colonial–style house. Most of these were lavishly illustrated with historical examples and recent interpretations, and they informed the reader not just about house style, but also about gardens, window treatments, and, generally, how to live. Some of these books attempted to address the problems of contemporary life and provide an antidote to the new modernism that appeared in these years. Nancy McClelland, writing in the mid-1930s, summed up the attraction: "If we can recapture from the past the homely and livable qualities of the old Colonial house; if we can translate into our modern dwellings its chief characteristics, its restfulness and sincerity, we shall have done something that is undoubtedly good for our souls in this heedless and hurried day and generation."[11]

The celebration of the quaint and the "Old Time" became a specialty of authors such as Wallace Nutting with his evocative photographs, and Robert and Elizabeth Shackleton, who produced such bestselling books as *The Quest of the Colonial* (1907) and *The Charm of the Antique* (1914). In these works they attempt to seduce the reader with images of the past: "An old clock ticked in the hall, and the leaping fire glimmered in the score of reflections in the room . . . as if to light all of us back into the glamour and the mystery of the past." Originally published in homemaker magazines such as *Good Housekeeping,* the work of the Shackletons fueled the growing antique market and also advised those who might, for instance, "have a house . . . [that] is not of the proper style." The solution, they said, was "only a matter of making it the proper style . . . the Colonial being a style, admirably adapted from the English, which fits alike the rich and the poor." When addressing matters specific to interior design, the Shackletons illustrated both "before" and "after" situations, and they highlighted the importance of the fireplace in the home: "People who learn to sit about fireplaces find their health improved, and their minds more at ease; they find more sociability, more friendliness, more genial tolerance, and a lightening and brightening of their lives."[12]

Some of these publications were prescriptive and instructed the reader as to what not to do, as in Joseph Everett Chandler's *The Colonial House* (1916). Chandler, who designed the Stevens-Coolidge House, often peppered his advice with historical facts, which he intended for those "who wish to avoid in their possible building operations, certain short-comings recognizable in much of the supposedly-in-the-old vein modern work."[13]

Emily Post, who found great success with *Etiquette: The Blue Book of Social Usage* (1922), also wrote *The Personality of a House: The Blue Book of Home Design and Decoration* (1930). The daughter of the well-known New York architect Bruce Price, himself a designer of numerous Colonial Revival–style houses, Post acknowledged many house styles in her book, including Colonial Revival and "Modern." Her thoughts on the latter left little room for misinterpretation: "[The] con-

tradictions of Modern design are more than confusing . . . [and is characterized by frequent suggestions of] cemetery monuments and mortuary chambers . . . [or] an asylum for the insane." At nearly five hundred pages, Post's book offered not only opinion, but also a wealth of practical information such as details on how to remodel a house. The style she preferred, though, was Colonial Revival, about which she wrote, "All good examples of Colonial houses are direct copies of the Classic orders . . . [and] for more than two thousand years every student of architecture has gone to the Classic orders." Moreover, most of the photographs in Post's book were of Colonial Revival–style interiors that had been done by leading architects.

THE COLLECTOR'S LAIR: HENRY DAVIS SLEEPER AND BEAUPORT

During the summer of 1907, Henry Davis Sleeper visited Emily and Elise Tyson at Hamilton House in South Berwick, Maine. Sleeper was so inspired by what he saw, especially the recently completed garden cottage and the reused old paneling, that when he returned to nearby Gloucester, Massachusetts, he set about purchasing fragments of old houses and creating his own retreat.[14]

By the early part of the twentieth century, the study of American antiques, or Early American decorative arts, was becoming professionalized. The opening of Pendleton House at the Rhode Island School of Design in 1906 and the installation of period rooms at the Essex Institute in Salem in 1907 were indicative of this change. Two years later, in 1909, the Hudson-Fulton Celebration at the Metropolitan Museum of Art in New York took place, marking the first major museum exhibition of Early American antiques. In 1924, the Metropolitan opened the American Wing.[15]

By 1907, Sleeper began construction of Beauport, utilizing materials such as paneling that had been removed from the eighteenth-century Cogswell House in nearby Essex, Massachusetts. Accompanying him on one of his research visits to the Cogswell House was Isabella Stewart Gardner (also known as "Mrs. Jack"), the creator of the Gardner Museum in Boston. Beauport, in a sense, was a sibling of the Gardner Museum, a collection of exquisite American-related objects, a sort of a bric-a-brac-mania assemblage. Isabella Gardner liked to surround herself with intelligent, artistically inclined, and precocious young men who were frequently gay.

Henry Davis Sleeper fit Mrs. Jack's model. Born in 1878 in Boston to a wealthy family, Sleeper suffered from poor health as a child and was privately tutored. He was only thirteen

ABOVE: Henry Davis Sleeper, Beauport, Gloucester, Massachusetts, 1907–34. Entrance facade.

OVERLEAF: Beauport. West facade and garden.

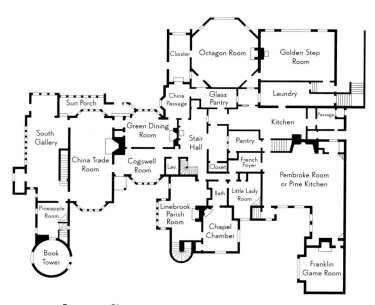

when his father died in 1891, and he lived with his mother until her death in 1917. He displayed an early interest in art, creating at the age of eleven a model of a Japanese garden. From his mother he acquired a taste for antique shopping. Although he never trained as an architect, he learned from his surroundings and from architect Arthur Little, who designed a summer house for Sleeper's parents in nearby Marblehead in 1889. Little encouraged him to work as a designer, and by the 1920s Sleeper had acquired a substantial group of wealthy clients across the United States. He

designed interiors and advised on antiques and, eventually, became popular with Hollywood personalities such as Frederic March. Sleeper also worked with Henry Francis du Pont on his first house on Long Island, and, later, at Winterthur in Delaware. In 1934, just before his death, Sleeper was elected as an honorary member of the AIA in recognition of his accomplishments.

Beauport, the house that Sleeper began in 1907 and altered continually into the 1930s, could be characterized as a hodgepodge of towers, gables, roof forms, and materials. Its aesthetic is almost playful, as if Hansel and Gretel were expected there. The historian might claim that features such as the clipped gable, the Palladian window, the overhangs, the spindle balconies, and the extended form, among other elements, reference the colonial past—and certainly they do— but Beauport's importance lies not on the outside but on the inside. The additive quality of the exterior reflects the interior and its creator's passion for American antiques. A friend of Sleeper's recalled him as saying, "Mightn't it be fun to have a house in which each room could recapture some of the spirit of a specific mood or phase or 'period' of our American life from the time of Plymouth down through the Revolution and the early Republic?"[16]

At Beauport, Sleeper worked with a local builder, Halfdan H. Hanson, who, under Sleeper's guidance, later opened an office as an architect and achieved some success. They frequently worked together on Sleeper's various commissions. Hanson certainly contributed to the success of Beauport,

both in construction and also in reconciling the different additions, but Sleeper was the main designer. Also assisting were local craftsmen such as Frederick Poole, who built many of the house's interior elements.

Of Beauport's forty rooms, several are worth examining. In the Pembroke Room—also called the Pine Kitchen because of its unpainted pine paneling, some of which came out of the Barker House (ca. 1650) in Pembroke, Massachusetts—Sleeper created the quintessential New England hearth. In addition to windows, the room has a skylight. Cupboards and tabletops are filled with jugs, dishes, plates, cutlery, and other utilitarian objects. Exemplifying the range of Sleeper's design interests, the China Trade Room is a two-story space that, in 1923, he covered with a set of hand-painted Chinese wallpapers, originally owned by Robert Morris, an eighteenth-century Philadelphia banker and patriot. Sleeper furnished the room with Chinese furniture. Later, in the 1930s, the house's new owners, Mr. and Mrs. Charles E. F. McCann, working in conjunction with the New York decorating firm of French and Company, replaced Sleeper's furniture with pieces of Chinese Chippendale and chinoiserie-styled items. Spaces such as the Octagon Room,

ABOVE: Beauport. Golden Step room.

BELOW: Beauport. Mariner's room.

TOP: Beauport. Bedroom.

BOTTOM: Beauport. Indian room.

with its eighteenth-century French pieces, reflect the Revolutionary alliance of France and America. The Indian Room and Porch, with its native American and folk art furnishings, represent Sleeper's multiple intentions.

At Beauport, Sleeper combined elements of old buildings with new display techniques. One of his signature elements was a window with shelves that contained displays of glass and antique bottles. Sleeper excelled at collecting odd objects from all periods and juxtaposing them. A critic observed in 1929: "This house is paramount perhaps as a composition. Its creator is more than a mere collector. He is more than an antiquarian. He is at heart an artist."[17]

Sleeper had an aesthete's appreciation of objects and forms no matter their sources. While the house was intended as a summer and weekend retreat, it often performed double duty as a demonstration space, a virtual architectural sales pitch for potential clients. Sleeper created a broader and

richer interpretation of "Early American" and demonstrated how multiple sources could be combined into a new artistic whole. In 1942, Beauport passed to SPNEA, which continues to preserve Sleeper's vision.

SEARS, ROEBUCK AND COMPANY'S COLONIAL FOR THE MIDDLE AND WORKING CLASSES

During the mid-1910s, Dr. Maurice and Mrs. Martha Watson decided to build a summer house in the small village of Gilmanton, which was located about forty miles north of their home in the large mill town of Manchester, New Hampshire. Settled in 1761, Gilmanton developed as a small yet prosperous crossroads town for the local farmers and gentry. An academy was established there and houses of varying sizes (built between 1770 and 1840) lined the town's two main roads. Many of the larger houses had elegant Georgian- and Federal-style detailing, while the smaller homes retained a chaste simplicity. By the 1840s, almost all the houses had been painted white, which is the color they remained. The town's fortunes declined after the Civil War, when many farmers gave up tilling the tough New England soil and departed for new land out West. As the concept of vacations caught on and individuals and families escaped the heat and pressure of rapidly growing cities, a summertime-retreat economy gradually replaced the one driven by farming. Summer residents usually boarded with people in town, or rented or purchased a house.[18] A few new houses were also built during this period, including the Watson House.

For their house, the Watsons consulted the catalog *Modern Homes,* which was produced by Sears, Roebuck and Company.[19] From the approximately twenty houses shown, they selected a gambrel-roofed model. Between 1911 and 1939, gambrel-roofed houses were plentiful in the Sears catalog; they had at least twenty-eight different versions. Both the English and Dutch colonists had at one time employed the gambrel roof—the Dutch linkage apparent in model names such as the Amsterdam, the Van Dorn, the Rembrandt, and the Van Page. Other names for gambrel houses included the Oak Park and the Newbury. Gambrel models with American names—the Martha Washington, the Puritan, the Amherst, the Salem, and the Newbury—were also common and were some of their best sellers.

Sears employed independent architects and builders to handle design. Some were brought on to produce a few standard models. Later, in 1919, Sears established its own architectural division, though designers' names remained anonymous. Stylistically, the Sears houses followed the popular tastes of

the day such as variations on the bungalow, the English cottage, the American foursquare, and of course colonial idioms. Sears initially thought that their market would desire very low-cost models, homes in the range of $400 to $1,500. Many of the models offered were designed to serve as cottages and second homes. Identification of style did not count for much in the early catalogs, but a description of a 1908 concrete-block house mentions: "The front porch has colonial columns." In the catalog's first years, Sears simply used model numbers to identify the houses, but by 1913 names began to appear. By 1920, at least one quarter of the houses shown in the catalog could be roughly defined as Colonial Revival in style. Number 2089, called the Magnolia, appeared between 1918 and 1921 and was described in the catalog as resembling Henry Wadsworth Longfellow's house in Cambridge. Sears also produced several variations on the Mission style, the most popular being number 2090, the Alhambra. In the 1930s, they produced the Jefferson, number 3349, which, according to the catalog copy that accompanied its promotion, had been "designed along the same lines as historic Mount Vernon, and is a true example of Southern Colonial architecture." This model wrapped the nation's first and third presidents into the same bundle. Sears went on to adopt Mount Vernon as its image, constructing full-scale reproductions for

OPPOSITE, TOP: Dr. Maurice Watson House, Gilmanton, New Hampshire, 1915. East facade.

OPPOSITE, BOTTOM: Watson House. View from southeast.

ABOVE: Watson House. Kitchen.

BELOW: Watson House. Living room.

Watson House. Kitchen.

Watson House. Dining room.

the 1931 international exposition in Paris and the 1931 Washington Bicentennial in Brooklyn.[20]

The Watsons selected model number 264P252, which was identified in the catalog as "a colonial home that is fast becoming popular." Later called the Adams model, its promotion copy claimed: "With its seven rooms, each having windows at least on two sides, bath, numerous closets, grade entrance, large vestibule, popular long living room and numerous conveniences, the Adams will give you solid comfort. Standing on the brick steps you face a porch and entrance of pure colonial lines with front door and sidelights—all in spotless white. Lovers of colonial architecture will surely fancy this house."[21] Similar models were the Martha Washington, said to be "a design that will delight lovers of the real colonial type of architecture," and the Rembrandt, "an unusually well arranged Dutch Colonial house."[22]

The Sears version of "Dutch Colonial" differed greatly from Washington Irving's earlier interpretation of the style. The focus here was on the gambrel roof. Although gambrel roofs had appeared in the 1880s and were not associated with the Dutch colonists, books and articles in the early 1900s began to assert its Dutch origin. Aymar Embury, a New York–based architect who published several books, including *The Dutch Colonial House* (1913), claimed that, for the small American house, "there is probably no other style so good." The American public, Embury asserted, desires a "long low house," and "it is not very difficult to secure the effect of a rather long, low house by the use of a gambrel roof starting at the second floor line." Embury admitted that "Dutch Colonial" was far removed from the genuine article but he suggested that it fit perfectly with the American penchant for dwellings that are "homelike, quaint and lovely."[23]

Although Sears catalogs labeled houses such as the Adams model "pure colonial," the look of the Watsons' Sears house differed significantly from Gilmanton's older, in many cases real eighteenth-century homes. Set well back from the road, instead of up close, as were all the early houses, the Watsons had a gambrel roof, which had never before appeared in Gilmanton. The porch, attached to one end, spoke of summer but was a feature seldom seen in early New Hampshire buildings. The front windows were placed close together in banks, rather than as separate elements—the common placement in most colonial-era houses.

The plans of most of the Sears houses were simple and boxlike or, in the case of the models the Watsons looked at, rectangular. A 1926 Sears house catalog showed how a "Colonial" might be furnished.[24] With the Sears houses, one could customize certain features such as the arrangement of the rooms, which could be reversed, and make changes to the entrance. It was even possible to take the facade from one house and combine it with the plan from another. The Watsons placed the large living room on the south side, and the dining and kitchen on the north, along with the porch. This allowed light to flood the living room from three sides. They also added a fireplace in the dining room. Sears provided high wainscoting and simple Colonial Revival mantels for the major spaces. They also provided kitchen cabinets, which, following the style of the day, were issued varnished, not painted. Upstairs were three bedrooms, one large and two small, and a bath. Since most of Gilmanton still relied on the outdoor privy, this was a real modern element. The Watsons' Sears house provided comfort, efficiency, and a hint of the colonial past, but without pretense. It was the high-grade package, one with better materials and heavy framing. It had a double floor and a hardwood surface of oak or maple. The house's lumber, details, nails, screws, plumbing, bathroom fixtures, asphalt shingles, and paint—all stamped by Sears—were shipped by railroad to the Watsons. (Bricks and concrete blocks, items that could be purchased locally, were not shipped.) The Watsons received their house via the Boston-Maine Railroad, at either the Belmont terminal (about seven miles away), or the Laconia depot (about twelve miles away), since Gilmanton lacked train service. Either trucks, or more probably several horse- or ox-drawn teams, brought the crates of materials to the building site alongside the Ironworks Road where a local carpenter, probably Dick Varney, built it.

Sears called the Watsons' Adams model a "Ready-Cut House," one that had been "Honor-Built," meaning it was the top of the line. Sears also offered more modest packages called "Standard Built Houses" and "Simplex," which employed lesser materials and frequently were used as summer or resort homes.

Prefabricated homes and buildings were not a new phenomenon of the twentieth century. Many of the buildings that made up Britain's nineteenth-century colonial empire came from England, and small prefabricated houses were shipped around the horn to the California gold fields in the mid-nineteenth century. Prefabricated building elements such as ornament, mill-worked balusters, cabinets, and plumbing and lighting supplies were a standard of nineteenth-century building practice and were supplied through local lumberyards and mail-order catalogs. Founded in 1886 in Chicago, Sears, Roebuck and Company had become the leading mail-order catalog company in the world with a significant amount of their business involved in selling homebuilding elements, from sinks and lamps to ornamental trim, or as their 1910 catalog put it, "Colonial columns" for both interior and exterior.[25]

The building materials department of Sears eventually encountered significant competition, especially from the Aladdin Company, which had introduced kit homes. Sears cast about for a solution, in the end turning to Frank W. Kushel, who was given the challenge of either reinvigorating the department or unloading it. Kushel came up with a concept that involved offering the parts for a house in a coordinated package, much like Aladdin's program. In 1908, Sears sent out the forty-four page *Book of Modern Homes and Building Plans,* which offered twenty-two houseplans that could be built from millwork and other components. The public responded enthusiastically. Sears also raised the stakes by

offering loan packages to the potential buyer at a time when most houses were sold on a cash basis. The terms were flexible—twenty-five percent down and varying interest rates for five to fifteen years—and the application form did not ask about ethnicity, gender, or race. In theory, the potential homeowner could build a Sears house by himself, though most houses were ultimately erected by professional builders (still, the savings remained great—sometimes up to forty percent).[26]

The exact number of Sears houses erected remains unknown; estimates vary between 50,000 to more than 100,000. Single houses were supplied, but there were also entire subdivisions of Sears houses that were established by local developers. Not necessarily inexpensive, some of them were advertised as "strictly high class."[27] The Sears house owned by the Watsons of Gilmanton is demonstrative of how the larger American public got their Colonial Revival house.

JOSEPH EVERETT CHANDLER: ENHANCING THE PAST

In 1914, Helen Stevens-Coolidge and her sisters jointly inherited the family's farm—eighty-nine acres and a house—at North Andover on the North Shore of Massachusetts. She and her husband, John Gardner Coolidge, promptly bought

Joseph Everett Chandler, Stevens-Coolidge House, North Andover, Massachusetts, 1914–30s (additions and alterations to house and grounds originally dating from ca. 1830–50). West facade.

out the sisters and set about creating a suitable country place.[28] Eight generations earlier, in 1633, her ancestors arrived from England and settled in the area. The Stevenses prospered as farmers, and between 1810 and 1830 they constructed a large frame house with brick ends along one of North Andover's main roads, a few hundred yards from the town common, with a tavern attached to one end of the house. Farming began to give out around 1850, and while the Stevens family continued to own the house, now their livelihood came from Boston. Later generations of the Stevens family "Victorianized" the house, replacing the hipped roof with a gabled roof, adding a large front gable, along with dormers, brackets, porches, a projecting entrance, ornamental trim, and a polychrome paint scheme. Although Helen Stevens came from an old family, her father's debilitating illness and his death in 1891, when she was only fifteen, left her without the income necessary for Boston society. She served as a companion to several wealthy Boston Brahmin ladies and eventually met and married John Gardner Coolidge, in 1909, at the age of thirty-three. Coolidge came from old, aristocratic, and moneyed Boston. (His relative John Gardner was married to Isabella Stewart Gardner of the Gardner Museum; and Coolidge was a great-great-grandson of Thomas Jefferson.) After Harvard College, Coolidge studied landscape gardening and then became a diplomat with posts in China, South Africa, Japan, Mexico, and Nicaragua. During a portion of World War I, the Coolidges were in Paris, where he served as a special agent for Turkish refugees living in Paris. While in Paris, they met Edith Wharton and Helen had the opportunity to admire the decoration of her apartment.[29]

For the transformation of the old Stevens house in North Andover, the Coolidges engaged Joseph Everett Chandler. John Coolidge described Chandler as "a little man . . . amiable and intelligent," adding, "he never says no to any suggestion; if he does not like it he seeks to divert it by oblique opposition."[30] The project began in 1914 and continued into the late 1930s, with Mrs. Coolidge more concerned about the house and Mr. Coolidge more focused on the gardens and landscaping. This was their country place, used during the summers and at holidays (they maintained a large house in Boston's Back Bay area as well). John Coolidge died in 1936, and at the time of Helen Stevens-Coolidge's passing in 1962, the property passed to the Trustees of Reservations, the organization that maintains it to this day.

Chandler, who was born in 1864 in Plymouth to a family who traced their lineage back to the Mayflower, studied

Stevens-Coolidge House. South facade.

architecture at the Massachusetts Institute of Technology, had worked for Little & Browne, and directed restoration of the House of the Seven Gables in Salem, Paul Revere's house, and the Old State House in Boston, and had also designed new buildings. He also wrote articles in *The White Pine Series* and published several books on Early American architecture. During his initial work at the Stevens-Coolidge House, Chandler published *The Colonial House* (1916), which he considered a corrective to the overly elaborate Colonial Revival work then going on. He also theorized, "The houses of our forefathers bespoke a fearless honesty characteristic of themselves—a lack of pretense and sham." He wanted, as he put it, the "rank and file of our nation . . . [to] return . . . toward this simplicity and again live a life approximating the sane life of our Colonial forebears." But, he elaborated, "it would be foolish in the extreme, and a detriment, to forego such modern and luxurious details as the telephone, electric lights and numerous modern improvements." For Chandler, the Colonial Revival style was "the best" because it was "adaptable to the needs of the better class of our people." Chandler believed in an American elite, who with proper education should control taste and architectural style.[31]

At the Stevens-Coolidge House, Chandler wiped out the Victorian modifications and transformed it into a house that might have been built around 1790–1800, though equipped with modern comforts. He described his intentions: "There will be new porch cornice, pediment, columns, pilasters, etc., exactly according to detail drawing, to be done in good white pine."[32] He added an elegant dentiled cornice at the roofline, removed the front gable, added quoins and a new central dormer with a scrolled pediment, installed Georgian windows and shutters, and replaced the Victorian projecting and bracketed porch with a suitably Georgian model. At either side, Chandler exposed the original brick ends, but, when it was determined that they were deteriorated, covered them with a new brick veneer. At the rear of the house, a bow window with French doors was added to the living room. Several shedlike additions were removed and the former tavern was renewed to be more in accord with the original house. Instead of the polychrome paint scheme, Chandler specified white paint.

Inside the house, Chandler opened spaces, integrating the front and rear stairs into a landing at the second level. Federal-style trim and moldings were added to the hall, and Joseph Remidas, a painter, created a set of murals. At the lower level, the murals depicted a garden, while upstairs cityscapes appeared. Remidas also painted the ballroom of

Stevens-Coolidge House. North facade and garden.

Stevens-Coolidge House. Sitting room.

the tavern wing in a more specifically colonial theme, that is, in sepia and color, creating the effect of a dream world. Other interior changes included the new bowed end of the living room, and a major extension of the dining room. The original dining room was quite small, so Chandler combined two rooms, and added a Dutch door at one side and, to enhance the room's appearance, replicated some paneling. The original fireplace and mantel were replaced with Chandler's new design, which included Delft tiles.

The Coolidges furnished the house with a mixture of American antiques and items that John Gardner Coolidge had collected during his various diplomatic postings. His collection of oriental porcelains reflects his connection to the china trade of the North Shore area. Mrs. Coolidge concentrated

RIGHT: Stevens-Coolidge House. Tavern.

OPPOSITE: Stevens-Coolidge House. Kitchen.

more on American antiques and frequently purchased furniture and other items from antique shops and auctions.[33]

On the grounds, Chandler made extensive improvements. The Coolidges desired to operate the estate as a model farm (they eventually raised prize-winning Guernsey cattle). The barn near the house was moved and Chandler made several additions to it. A garden planned and planted by Mrs. Coolidge's sister in 1907 that opened off the living room received a semicircular addition to reflect the bow window Chandler had added to the house. Adjacent to it, Chandler designed a sunken rose garden in 1926. The garden was located on the site of the old barn and pigsty, and John Coolidge wrote in his diary that the area would be "turned into a sunken walled garden full of delicious smells."[34] Later, Chandler made some adjustments to accommodate several French garden ornaments that Mrs. Coolidge had purchased. The last major design for the house was the French garden, an effort that began in 1931. Intended to memorialize Mr. Coolidge's relationship to Thomas Jefferson, a serpentine brick wall, as employed at the University of Virginia, served as a backdrop for thirty-six beds of perennials and annuals. Designed on a skewered axis, the garden, like the house, was a mixture of historical recall and romantic sensibility.

ABOVE, LEFT: Stevens-Coolidge House. Bedroom.

LEFT: Stevens-Coolidge House. Entrance hall staircase.

ABOVE, RIGHT: Stevens-Coolidge House. Detail of wall painting in entrance hall.

Stevens-Coolidge House. French garden.

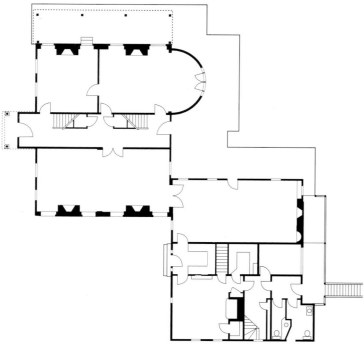

TOP: Stevens-Coolidge House. French garden.

LEFT: Stevens-Coolidge House. Plan.

ABOVE: Stevens-Coolidge House. Sunken rose garden.

The Coolidges became enamored of North Andover and attempted to create a proper colonial village there. They purchased land adjacent to their house and stopped a major highway from entering the town. Chandler "Colonialized" a house on the property for use by the staff. The "historical" town common was a recent creation, the product of the North Andover Town Improvement Society. Since 1885, plans had been underway to create a common, and Mrs. Coolidge purchased land and houses around it. She later demolished the more unsightly houses among them, and engaged Chandler to enhance the colonial character of others. Mrs. Coolidge opened a tearoom in one of the houses, and Chandler drew up a plan for the common with plantings and statuary. But the town rejected it, favoring an irregular and more picturesque space. Although not all of Chandler and Coolidge's plans were carried out, they partially succeeded in enhancing the colonial character of the town.

WALLACE NUTTING: EMBELLISHING THE REAL

Wallace Nutting had a multifaceted career. He began as a Congregational minister and eventually became a spokesman for early America through his photography, commerce, manufacturing, writing, collecting, and preservation activities. His color photographs of staged scenes in Early American houses and his series of travel books have already been mentioned. He also amassed one of the most comprehensive collections of Early American furniture, authored two of the most important books on that subject—*Furniture of the Pilgrim Century* (1921) and the three-volume *Furniture Treasury* (1928–33)—and ran a large furniture-making enterprise that reproduced—and sold with great profit—Early American furniture. His catalogs railed against contemporary styles: "The interior desecration of America has proceeded apace since 1800, each succeeding decade worse than that which preceded it." He believed that Early American furniture, even if replicated, invoked the "strength and beauty in the character of the leaders." Hence, he came up with the maxim: "Copy, and avoid bad taste. Not all the old is good but all the new is bad."[35] To promote his commercial endeavors, he created the Wallace Nutting Chain of Colonial Picture Houses. The houses were elaborated visions for tourists of what old New England should look like.

RIGHT: Wallace Nutting and Henry Charles Dean, Broadhearth, Saugus, Massachusetts, 1915 (restoration of house originally built ca. 1680). Detail of entrance.

OVERLEAF: Broadhearth. Entrance facade.

Nutting's initial foray—and his most dramatic restoration—was the Ironworks House in Saugus, Massachusetts, also known as the Appleton-Taylor-Mansfield House, or, as Nutting rechristened it, Broadhearth. William Sumner Appleton, then the director of SPNEA, brought the house to Nutting's attention but with the proviso that Nutting would turn the house over to the SPNEA after, as Appleton put it, "doing nothing to it except what our experience has taught us is the proper thing to do to such a house." He did not want it "over repaired or wrongly repaired, or restored to something very attractive indeed."[36] The projected collaboration failed because Appleton's purist preservation philosophy conflicted with Nutting's approach of commercialism and historic embellishment.

In early March 1915, Nutting purchased the house and commenced with the architect Henry Charles Dean to remove the various facades, roof, and other features that had been added since the house was originally built. Dean, a Boston architect who specialized in colonial-era design and restoration, was part of the Browne-Chandler group. He

produced a design that, while faithful to the basic form, overemphasized certain details. The house was taken apart to its frame, and new clapboards were added. Major exterior features, such as the projecting porch and twin gables, inspired by North Shore houses such as the recently restored House of the Seven Gables in Salem, were apparently figments of Nutting and Dean's imagination, since question marks appear on Dean's drawings. Essentially, they created the quintessential New England seventeenth-century house, complete with a dramatic overhang, finials, and a projecting porch.[37]

Nutting and Dean assigned the date of "about 1640" to the house, though later research tends to favor around 1680.[38] The 1640 date was important to Nutting, as he wanted the house to be considered one of, if not the, oldest in the area. The Fairbanks-Morse House in Dedham (1636) was, however, commonly acknowledged as the earliest wood-frame house standing in New England.

Entranced with the house's history, especially the fact that it was once part of an iron works, Nutting purchased nearby buildings and set up a blacksmith shop to produce versions of historic iron details. He hired Edward Guy, a "descendent of a

ABOVE: Broadhearth. View prior to restoration.

BELOW: Broadhearth. West facade.

line of forgemen of five generations," and promoted ironwork as a romantic survivor of a period when the "age of chivalry had passed away and the modern-time machinery had not come in." Unfortunately, the ironworks proved less than successful. After failed attempts at selling it to SPNEA, Nutting finally sold it to an antiques dealer. In the 1950s, a new interest in the industrial past led the American Iron and Steel Institute to acquire the site and create a "faithful replica" of an early iron mill. The National Park Service inherited the complex in 1968 and operates it today as the Saugus Ironworks National Historic Site.[39] Portions of the interior of the house have been "re-restored."

Of the four other houses that Nutting purchased for his chain, the Joseph Webb House, alternately referred to as Hospitality Hall, and also as the Webb-Deane-Stevens House, in Wethersfield, Connecticut, most embellishes the past. Built in 1752 for Joseph Webb, a merchant, the house was a large weatherboarded, five-bayed, gambrel-roofed structure sited on an elm-tree-lined main street in a historically evocative town. A substantial house for its period, it became the center of the town's social activity during the Revolutionary War—hence its name, Hospitality Hall. Also, Washington had slept there. The most important visit occurred in mid-May 1781, when Washington and his staff met with the comte de Rochambeau and plotted the campaign that resulted a few months later in the surrender of Lord Cornwallis at Yorktown and the effective end of the War for Independence. Later owners largely maintained the house, though at one point the kitchen was modified and a new entrance porch was added around 1821. The interior received some new mantels and moldings. The house gained substantial fame through the years, and in 1915 Appleton of SPNEA pressured Nutting to buy the house.

Nutting purchased the house in February 1916 and set about making repairs. A headline in the *Hartford Daily*

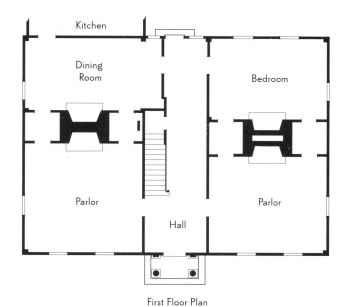

First Floor Plan

Wallace Nutting, Hospitality Hall, Wethersfield, Connecticut, 1916. Plan.

Courant read, "ARTIST TAKES IT BACK TO OLD DAYS." The article explained Nutting "spent many thousands of dollars in improving it, so that the interior, at least, looks almost as it did during the Colonial period." The Greek Revival–style porch, which gave a classical air to the house, was retained. Inside the house, substantial work was done on the kitchen ell, which was thought—inaccurately according to later research—to have been revamped earlier. Nutting's mason, E. A. Smith, rebuilt the fireplaces in the ell, in addition to installing a brick floor. Nutting preserved many original elements, such as the red floral wallpaper in the best bedroom (called the "Washington Chamber") on the second floor, though Nutting wrote, "We cannot claim anything for its beauty, but, of course it would not be proper to disturb it."[40]

Nutting respected parts of the house's original interior, but he also embellished. For the central hall, he commissioned a mural depicting British castle scenes and landscapes. The dining room had been remodeled at some point, and Nutting ripped out the mantel and paneling and replaced it with a corner cupboard, mantel, and paneling from a recently demolished Wethersfield house that had originally been built for a Reverend John Marsh. When his project carpenter, G. W. Dodge, replaced some moldings without first obtaining

Wallace Nutting, hand-tinted platinum print of Yorktown Parlor at Hospitality Hall, ca. 1916.

Hospitality Hall. Garden.

Nutting's approval, Nutting wrote, "I have gotten through employing him."[41] A wallpaper treatment depicting a landscape scene, decidedly unoriginal, was also installed. The northeast parlor, which contained the most elaborate woodwork, including a built-in cupboard, was preserved, but the walls received a mural of Early American country roads, bridges, and several houses, including Broadhearth and others. Nutting literally painted his commercial and preservation efforts into history.

The southeast sitting room received the most extensive renovation. By tradition, it was known as the "Yorktown parlor," though no evidence existed that the meetings actually took place in that room. The mantel had been replaced around 1821, though Nutting thought it dated it to around 1870. He tore it out, explaining: "I have a beauty of the period of the house (1745–50) with fine scroll top which I am putting in."[42] For the walls, Nutting hired three muralists from Hartford—Walter Korder, Louis Donlon, and Edwin Yungk—who portrayed Washington and his staff meeting with the French, their subsequent march down the East Coast, their battle, and the surrender of the British at Yorktown. He filled the house with notable antiques and some of his own reproductions. On the floor, he used braided rugs, which his wife, Marie, made and he sold. Such rugs were a post–Civil War invention, which, by the turn of the century, had become closely identified with the colonial period.

Nutting originally paid $3,000 for the house. By 1919, he

LEFT: Hospitality Hall. East facade.

OVERLEAF: Hospitality Hall. West facade and garden.

had spent an additional $3572.09 on building expenses and utilities. Unfortunately for Nutting, the commercial return on the house proved to be negligible, due in large part to the United States's entry into World War I and the consequential death of tourism in the country. He then sold the house, along with the others he had acquired during the period. The Colonial Dames of America acquired Hospitality Hall.

The Colonial Dames enlisted J. Frederick Kelly, a well-known Connecticut preservationist and historian of early architecture, to assess the property. He dismissed the murals as juvenile, and most of them were painted over. The Rhode Island mantel was removed and sold to a New York antiques dealer, who subsequently sold it to Henry Francis Dupont for installation at Winterthur. A number of years later, Nutting, perhaps smarting from this removal, wrote: "The acquisition of old paneling and its installation in rooms which perhaps never had any, is legitimate. If the dwelling is substantial there is nothing but praise in the effort to give it a good old dress." Although the Colonial Dames removed some of Nutting's work, they also commissioned certain new works for the house. In 1921, Amy Cogswell of Norwich, Connecticut, and a graduate of the Lathrop School of Horticulture for

ABOVE, LEFT: Hospitality Hall.

LEFT: Hospitality Hall. Entrance hall.

ABOVE, RIGHT: Hospitality Hall. Bedroom.

OPPOSITE: Hospitality Hall.

Hospitality Hall. Yorktown room.

Women, was hired to design a garden to the rear of the house. Cogswell's axial garden with rose trellises and period plantings represents what an eighteenth-century garden might have been like. In recent years, there have been attempts to restore the Nutting murals. [43]

DAVID ADLER AND THE COLONIAL OF CHICAGO'S NORTH SHORE

Most discussions of Chicago architecture, especially suburban houses, focus on the work of Frank Lloyd Wright and the Prairie School. Wright, as noted earlier, viewed Colonial Revival with antipathy, despite having experimented with several Colonial Revival variations in the late 1880s and early 1890s. In the mid-1890s, Wright expressed his dissatisfaction with Colonial Revival, attacking what he called the "wedding-cake artificiality of the Colonial pretense."[44]

In spite of—or perhaps because of—Wright's genius and polemics, Chicagoans supported a significant cadre of traditional architects, among whom David Adler stands at the head. Adler, capable of working in many different styles, concentrated almost exclusively on suburban and country houses and gained a national reputation for it. Many of his houses are located in Chicago's suburban North Shore area, where he designed two fine interwar Colonial Revival houses.

Born in 1882 in Milwaukee, where his family owned a men's clothing manufacturing company, Adler attended Princeton University and then studied architecture in

Hospitality Hall. Northeast parlor.

Munich and at the Ecole des Beaux-Arts in Paris. He returned to Chicago and worked briefly for Howard Van Doren Shaw, a prominent American architect. Beginning in 1911, and usually with a partner since he could not pass the registration examination, Adler began producing elegant, art-filled houses for wealthy Chicagoans. Adler initially employed French and Italian styles, but this changed in the 1920s when he discovered the pleasures of American colonial-era architecture. He possessed a large architectural library and his fastidiousness for detail became legendary. One draftsman recalled: "I was fascinated by Adler's sharp eye for detail and scale. He was a man who could come to the drafting board and see small-scale work, where we were working on plans sometimes as small as an eighth of an inch to the foot, and could discuss inches at that scale. It was a common thing if I were working, for example, at a larger scale, three inches to the foot on larger details, I would think nothing of being instructed to move a line a quarter of an inch at that scale because Adler saw a difference in proportion or expression." Adler's scientific-eclectic attitude was described by another draftsman: "The exactness of copying required a precise application of it to the project in hand: precise in scale, precise in period, precise in its relation to the project and to other selected details, precise also in having all the fullness and body of the original details. This was particularly true of the Georgian cornices and frames, their bolection molds and cyma reversas."[45]

Crab Tree Farm, the house and grounds Adler created between 1926 and 1928 for Helen Bowen and William McCormick Blair, represents Adler's facility at creating evocative images and handling detail. The owners came from old Chicago families, and they owned a large country estate that fronted Lake Michigan in Lake Bluff. Adler originally presented the Blairs with a Palladian-derived scheme consisting of a central block and balancing wings, but then they took a motoring trip up the East Coast, during which they inspected colonial-era structures. Adler was entranced with an extended Cape Cod–styled farmhouse at Old Westbury, owned by James Watson and Electra Havemeyer Webb, who also owned Shelburne Farm in Vermont and who were then avidly purchasing art and houses from the colonial and early American periods. Adler had numerous photographs taken of the farmhouse. [46]

The southern portion of the Blair House is a small Cape-styled structure with an addition and an ell, onto which a

David Adler, William McCormick Blair House, Lake Bluff, Illinois, 1926–28. Plan.

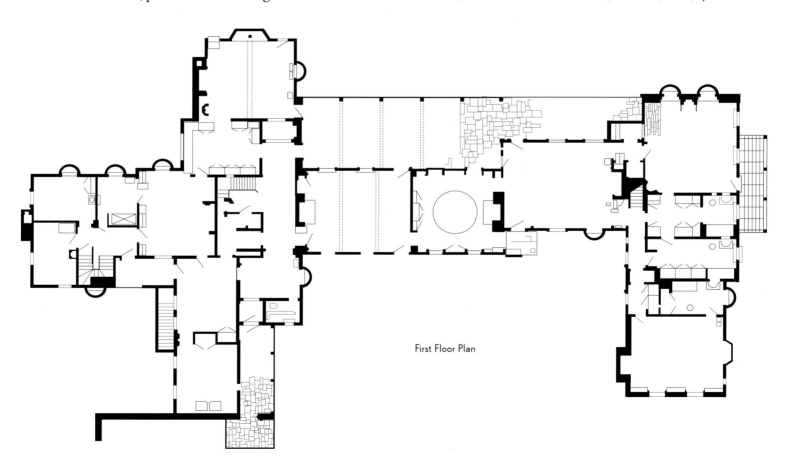

First Floor Plan

ABOVE: Blair House. West facade.

OVERLEAF: Blair House. View from southeast.

Blair House. Detail of dining room.

larger five-bay late-Georgian-style, or Federal-style, house appears to have been attached. To the latter, a barnlike structure was appended. The strung-out form with its multiple rooflines, variety of fenestrations, and contrasts of materials—from shingles to stone—looks like a building that has been added to and extended over the years. Certainly this is an interpretation that Adler anticipated. Matlack Price, writing for *Architectural Forum* in 1929, described the house: "It has achieved all the storied charm of a venerable ancestral home, traditioned through generations. . . . This house, for instance, gives the impression of a place of old and known abode, a place created by and a part of gentlefolk who lived here, who entertained here in a more leisurely age."[47] The small low-walled garden to the front added to this sense of age and accumulation. Designed by Ellen Biddle Shipman, the garden acted as an outdoor room and, in its clustered density, contained elements of what was identified as Colonial Revival.

One of the most creative elements of the house is Adler's shaping and use of space and procession. Access to the Blair House is through a forecourt but, instead of a central axis through the low garden wall to the door in the middle of the five-bayed house, one moves to the side and through the barn door into a loggia along the edge of the small garden. Once

Blair House. Sitting room.

Blair House. Pine room.

inside and through a small vestibule, the visitor's movement is along sight lines through a changing variety of spaces, each with its own decor. Views to the east of the green lawn—the trees, the blue of Lake Michigan, and the sky above—are a constant presence and a unifier of the procession. Inside, Adler's spatial sequencing, and indeed the entire picturesque composition, recalls Sleeper's Beauport, which he and the Blairs probably visited on their East Coast jaunt.

Adler, working in conjunction with Mrs. Blair, who was knowledgeable about interiors, looked carefully at various colonial sources. The entry hall's paneling is unpainted pine, fashioned in an eighteenth-century rural vernacular style. The paneling has recessed panels with frames that contained Mr. Blair's large collection of Currier & Ives prints. As a source for the dining room, Adler and Mrs. Blair chose the Hewlett Room—which was installed in the recently opened

BELOW: Blair House.

RIGHT: Blair House. Detail of dining room wall covering.

American Wing (1924) at the Metropolitan Museum of Art. The Hewlett Room was unbalanced because a built-in cupboard was located on only one side of the mantel; in Adler's version, a balancing cupboard was added and the unorthodox pilasters above the fireplace, which lacked a proper base, were omitted. The dining room also contained a bay window and French landscape wallpaper dating to the 1820s. The front hall's bay window displayed Mrs. Blair's collection of Early American glass; the source was, again, Sleeper's Beauport, as was the cool red paneling and the recessed ceiling of the library. The meticulous drawings by Adler's draftsmen reveal a passion for detail.

Adler's design for the Kersey Coates Reed House in nearby Lake Forest is very different from the Blair House and shows his comparable ability with large, formal neo-Georgian houses. Initial plans had been discussed in 1929; however, the death of Mr. Reed later that year necessitated some delay. By April 1931, construction had begun, and in 1932, Adler's sister, Frances Elkins, a noted interior designer, became heavily involved with selecting interior furnishings for the house. Mrs. Reed occupied the house later that year, and in 1934, it received the nod of approval from Augusta Owen Patterson, an authority on American country houses, who deemed it "clean and uncomplicated." Certainly an understatement for

ABOVE: David Adler, Kersey Coats Reed House, Lake Forest, Illinois, 1931–32. Plan.

OPPOSITE: Reed House. Main staircase.

a house that stretched 224 feet along a site overlooking Lake Michigan and contained many rooms. However, Adler's design exhibits an air of masterly control of proportions, an enfilade of spaces, and historical references.[48]

Stylistically, Adler drew upon Cliveden (1763–67), a venerable Germantown, Pennsylvania, house that was widely available to him in books. Pennsylvania micro-flecked fieldstone was imported for the exterior walls. For the form, Adler chose a Palladian five-part composition consisting of a central block, hyphens, wings, and a subordinate service wing. To tame

Reed House. West facade.

ABOVE: Reed House. Detail of Chinese Chippendale room.

BELOW: Reed House. Dining room.

such a large mass, Adler abstained from the usual detailing of pilasters, engaged columns, quoins, and grand pediment over the front door. Rather, the entrance treatment is subdued, and he shifted attention to the mass by the use of white marble headers and keystones over the main block's windows and white-painted shutters. In contrast, the garden elevation contains a far more elaborate entrance treatment, and the tall French window-doors lack headers.

In large houses, Adler liked to employ cross-axial halls as a means of uniting the different spaces. The entrance hall of this house, with its elaborate neo-Georgian moldings, door surrounds, trim, and large eagle-pedestal tables—recalling the work of Grinling Gibbons and also William Rush—leads to a gallery-stair-hall that stretched for eighty-three feet. This space is extended for another seventy feet by a living porch at one end and a hall and dining room at the other. The elliptical stair hall can be called modernized Colonial Revival with its graceful cantilevered staircase and classical detailing. Actually, Adler adapted it from a stair hall by John Russell Pope, but he enlivened it with ebony stair treads and a handrail, and the stair balusters, or spindles, are wrought glass.[49] An Adler trademark was dramatic and contrasting

ABOVE: Reed House. Chinese Chippendale room.

BELOW: Reed House. Ladies' powder room.

OVERLEAF: Reed House. West facade.

floor treatments, and, in various spaces, black-and-white marble is used along with wood patterns. Working with his sister, Francis Elkins, Adler designed and furnished in contrasting treatments that ranged from Chinese wallpaper to items associated with Art Deco and neo-Georgian. Several French decorators contributed to the mélange. A Colonial Revival sensibility was but part of the Reed House, which shows how a carefully selected colonial image could be a framework for a grand house.

RICHARD HENRY DANA AND THE NATIONAL SOCIETY FOR THE COLONIAL DAMES MUSEUM HOUSE

An important feature of the Colonial Revival mentality was the creation of organizations whose missions were to celebrate American history. Although some men belonged to and sometimes headed these groups, as with Appleton and SPNEA, women always played a key role and frequently created their own exclusive organizations such as the Daughters of the American Revolution (founded 1890), the Colonial

National Society of the Colonial Dames House. Entrance hall.

Dames of America (founded April 1891), and the National Society of Colonial Dames (founded June 1891). These organizations stressed lineage and tended to appeal to an elite section of the American population, many of whom worried about challenges to their status. They promoted patriotism, a selective view of American history, and the preservation of the colonial past. The historic houses supported by these groups include some of the most venerable, including Gunston Hall near Alexandria, Virginia; Wilton in Richmond, Virginia; the Moffatt-Ladd House in New Hampshire; and many more. They also were instrumental in restoring Sulgrave Manor, near Banbury, England, the ancestral home of George Washington.[50]

The headquarters building and museum house of the New

York City chapter of the National Society of Colonial Dames, built between 1928 and 1930, exemplifies the scientific eclecticism that dominated certain aspects of the Colonial Revival in the 1920s and 1930s. The New York chapter had for years cared for the venerable Van Cortlandt Mansion (1748), located in the Bronx, but they needed a building for meetings that would be located nearer to the center of social events on the Upper East Side of Manhattan. The membership, mostly members of New York's society, could afford an elegant re-creation of what colonial New York should have looked like. The chapter formed a committee whose members included the wives of Luke Vincent Lockwood, an important Early American antique collector, and R. T. H. Halsey, who supervised the period room installation and wrote the handbook for the Metropolitan Museum of Art's American Wing in 1924. Seeking an architect, the committee asked Halsey for a recommendation, and he responded with three names: William Adams Delano, William Lawrence Bottomley, and Richard Henry Dana Jr.[51]

OPPOSITE: Richard Henry Dana Jr., National Society of the Colonial Dames House, New York, New York, 1928–30.

Dana had the quintessential society practice, with notable houses and buildings in the period styles, including the Colonial Revival, throughout the Northeast. He came from venerable New England stock; his grandfather wrote *Two Years Before the Mast* (1840), and, on his mother's side, he was the grandson of Henry Wadsworth Longfellow. He grew up next door to Longfellow's house in Cambridge, attended the usual private schools before going to Harvard, and then studied architecture at Columbia University, followed by two years at the Ecole des Beaux-Arts. He worked for several New York design firms, including Delano & Aldrich, and in 1908, set up his practice in the city, where he remained until his death in 1933.[52]

In a letter to the chair of the building committee, Dana explained that he originally intended "to have all the details copied from old Colonial houses in New York State." But as "there are not enough of these still in existence," he said, he drew upon other states. He claimed that the architectural styles were "unusually uniform . . . owing to the fact that they [builders] all copied certain architectural books published in England."[53] The consequence was a design that liberally quotes from Dutch New York, as in the brickwork from the Schuyler Mansion in Albany, and the entrance door and fanlight from Philipse Manor Hall in Yonkers, though the scroll pediment over the door came from Westover on the James River in Virginia. The captain's walk was inspired by his grandfather's house in Cambridge. Inside the house, Dana's sources were equally diverse. The staircase was inspired by

National Society of the Colonial Dames House. Chinese reception room.

Sturgis's drawings of the John Hancock House in Boston. The entrance hall fireplace and overmantel were borrowed from the John Marsh House in Wethersfield, Connecticut, and the elliptical arch design can be traced to Carter's Grove in Virginia.

What sounds like a melange of elements actually worked, since Dana adapted and changed the scale of the different elements in order to unify them. Dana attributed some of his design decisions to other authorities such as "the Metropolitan Museum and Mr. Fiske Kimball."[54] Initially, Dana submitted a five-bayed symmetrical design but then rethought the proposal. Although he claimed that he took the facade from a long-demolished town house that originally stood at 34 Wall Street, the site on East Seventy-first Street was wider, and he added a bay. The result was an asymmetrical facade—approximately double the size of the original. Similarly, the interior was intended for twentieth-century social functions and, hence, the spaces aspire to Georgian elegance rather than the simplicity and intimacy of the colonial period. For two of the largest rooms, the ballroom and dining room, Dana resorted to importing elements from English buildings, since the Colonial Dames required a grander scale than American models could supply. The dining room contained a carved mantel, overmantel, and china closets derived from Holly Wells, Ipswich, England. The library had a mantel from Portland Place House in London. The grand ballroom had an original mantel and overmantel from the Mercer's Guild Hall in York, England, dating to 1760. Dana copied this model for the opposite end, adopted the Palladian window from Mount Pleasant in Philadelphia, based the minstrels gallery on the balustrades from the Vassall-Craigie-Longfellow House in Cambridge, and, for the mirrors, utilized drawings from the Isaac Royal House in Medford, Massachusetts. The design of the elegant black-and-white marble floor of the entrance hall was, according to Dana, borrowed from the Nelson House in Yorktown; however, he probably did not know that it was a replacement dating to around 1900.[55] Likewise, furnishings were varied, with American-made pieces by Paul Revere mixed with English furniture and objects.

ROLAND COATE AND THE VARIETIES OF THE SPANISH COLONIAL

By the mid-1910s, corresponding with the Eastern disparagement of giant-columnar Old Southern Colonial, the Mission

TOP: National Society of the Colonial Dames House. Reception room.

BOTTOM: National Society of the Colonial Dames House. Reception room.

Revival came under attack, with many seeing it as unsophisticated. A more academic perspective emerged based on a new interpretation of the Spanish colonial past. The California Tower and Administration Building at the Panama-California Exposition in San Diego in 1915, designed by East Coast architects Bertram Grosvenor Goodhue and Carleton Winslow, inaugurated the rage for more sophisticated and historical imagery—what was labeled *Spanish Colonial Revival.* The term covered a wide variety of idioms, or combinations of styles, that ranged from Spanish Baroque, or Churrigueresque, to Moorish or Islamic, Plateresque, Andalusian, Ranchero, Mediterranean, and Monterey Colonial. Buildings in these idioms ranged from the grandeur of Hearst Castle at San Simeon and the lavish Santa Barbara County Court House, to more modest structures. After the earthquake and fire of 1925, Santa Barbara adopted Spanish Colonial as the official style for all new construction.[56]

Supporting this new interpretation of the Spanish colonial past, in California in particular, were a host of publications addressed to all levels of architecture. William Lawrence Bottomley, who wrote *Spanish Details* (1924), and Arthur and Mildred Byne—who, between 1915 and 1927, authored seven books, including *Provincial Houses in Spain*—covered topics such as gardens, wooden ceilings, ironwork, and art. These and other publications helped spread the Spanish idiom across the country, not just to the former Spanish colonial areas such as the Southwest, Texas, and Florida, but to other parts of the United States as well. Although flamboyant designs appeared as part of the style, the underlying agenda was to create a structure more simple than that of the Mission Revival. Or, as the architect John Bakewell Jr. put it, a "style of early California . . . [which] might well have been constructed in the [nineteenth-century] towns of Los Angeles, Monterey or Santa Barbara as the city residence of a family of refinement. It is quite free from anything that savors of the clever 'stunt' of the false note of transported stage scenery. Simple, sincere, and chaste. . . ."[57]

Of the many talented California architects of the period, Roland E. Coate provided some of the subtlest interpretations of this revised view of the Spanish colonial past. Born in 1890 in Indiana, Coate graduated from the Beaux Arts–oriented architecture program at Cornell University in 1914, and, after a European tour, worked in Indiana, Washington, D.C., and then New York, before coming to Southern California and entering into a partnership with Reginald Johnson and Gordon Kaufmann. Together, they designed a variety of projects for the wealthy of Los Angeles and Pasadena. After they disbanded in 1925, Coate pursued a largely domestic practice, designing houses for several movie stars and a few churches. Coate also engaged in a polemical crusade, arguing that a unique California style could be found in the houses of Spain. In an article of 1929, Coate explained his thoughts on that relationship: "In California, the original borrowing was Spanish. . . . California houses were as nearly like the houses of Andalusia as the crudity of materials and dearth of workmen could make them. For it was the Spanish province of Andalusia which sent the first soldiers and adventurers to California."[58]

The house Coate designed for Mr. and Mrs. William Donaldson Edwards in San Marino, California, fits this description.[59] A retired couple living in Pasadena, they had purchased land in the elite residential enclave of San Marino, an adjacent town. Coate placed the house well back on the lot and gave it an entrance drive of 173 feet leading to a forecourt. A large restrained front facade of white stucco, a large central entrance, and a low-pitched red-tile roof greets the visitor. A single-story wing to one side contained a passage to the garages and service areas. The garages, hidden from public view, were constructed in a board-and-batten style, delineating their subsidiary function. Large blank wall surfaces of white stucco, exposed wooden timbers, small asymmetrically placed windows, and windows covered with iron grills gave the house a slightly fortified appearance that guarded against both unwelcome visitors and provided shelter in a warm climate. The house, both in form and plan, had an additive character, as if it had been built over several years. The entrance hall opened onto the patio to the rear; the floor was tiled, and doorways framed in Spanish tile

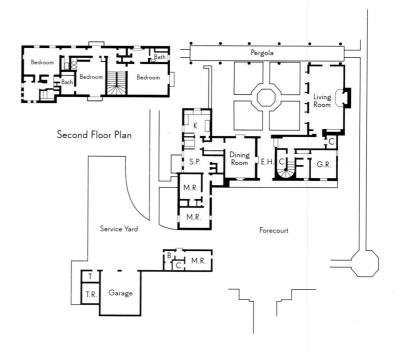

Roland E. Coate, William Donaldson Edwards House, San Marino, California, 1926–27. Plan.

Edwards House. Garden facade.

Roland E. Coate, Miss Katherine Lefens House, Pasadena, California, 1933.

gave access to the entertainment and living areas. The patio centered on a fountain, and gardens led down to a dry creek bed at the rear of the lot. In the living room, the fireplace was treated as a dark void in the white stucco walls, and the main emphasis was on the exposed-beam ceiling, which gave a rustic, or, as Californians called it, a "Ranchero" effect. Throughout the house, Coate provided custom-designed iron grills for the heating vents. He also chose red tile for the floors, which contrasted with hardwood in some rooms, and in certain small areas he specified decorative Spanish tile, some of it made locally. The Edwards House was completed in late 1925 at a cost of $25,135, plus architect's fees. Coate would return two years later to make an addition to the service wing.[60]

Lefens House. Entrance hall.

First Floor Plan

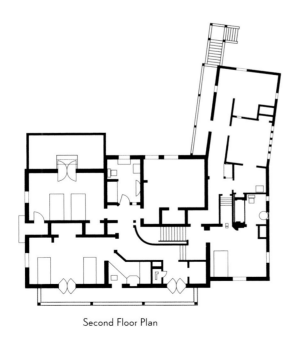

Second Floor Plan

By 1933, the Depression was well underway and restraint was in the air, even among those who could afford substantial houses. Thus, it seems logical that Coate's design of the Katherine Lefens House, completed that year, was subtle and carefully modulated. Coate's article of 1929 noted another source for contemporary design: "But when California became a member of the Union and officials, settlers and artisans came to the capital, Monterey, they found Spanish style not to their liking and they added to them details of New England Colonial houses." Coate was referring to several Monterey houses of the period 1830–50 that American settlers had modified in significant ways. He set the Lefens House back from the street with a white-painted low wall, and the house's facade carried a balcony across its full width. The balcony slates were cut in a heart-shaped pattern, unknown to the Spanish settlers but brought west by the migration of Easterners to California. Similarly, the front door was Federal style, complete with panels and sidelights. Placed on the north side, and helping to shelter the patio at the rear, was a wing covered in clapboards on one side and shingles on the other—a feature that would have fit a New England–styled Colonial Revival house. The patio facade contained a bay window for the dining room and a trellised porch that continued the heart pattern at the front.[61]

Inside the Lefens House, and in contrast to the through-hall of the Edwards House, one enters a generously proportioned hall and immediately confronts a New England–styled staircase rising perpendicular to the axis. The rest of the Lefens interior continues the theme of New England restraint. Mantels and moldings appear taken from the *White Pine Series* or pattern books by Asher Benjamin and others. The original

Lefens House. Plans.

TOP: Lefens House. Dining room.

BOTTOM: Lefens House. Living room.

interior decorators were Cheeswright, Mason & Company, and they supplied wing and side chairs imitative of Georgian and Federal styles and similar to what might have been imported with the early California settlers of the 1830s and 1840s.

VIRGINIA GEORGIAN:
WILLIAM LAWRENCE BOTTOMLEY

Virginia's large brick houses became one of the most popular and persistent Colonial design idioms. Frequently depicted in illustrations and described in prose as houses inhabited by elegantly costumed whites being served by black slaves, the myth of a gracious and genteel Old Dominion assumed a place of importance in the public imagination. Of the many architects who mastered the Virginia house form, while

accommodating modern requirements, William Lawrence Bottomley is the acknowledged master. He was the favorite architect of the Virginia elite in the decades of the 1910s, 1920s, and 1930s, receiving at least forty-seven commissions in the state, although he was a Northerner with an office in New York City. He explained his position in a 1929 interview: "I believe we should do everything possible to preserve this old southern ideal of a country house architecture because it is one of the finest things we have and it is still vital."[62]

Bottomley exuded a cosmopolitan air that made him particularly attractive to Southerners, who felt a need to combat their perceived provinciality. Born in New York City, he studied architecture at Columbia University and then at the Ecole des Beaux-Arts in Paris. In common with many of his academic New York contemporaries, he designed houses, clubhouses, apartment buildings, and public buildings, in a variety of idioms—including Spanish, Art Deco, and Georgian—throughout the mid-Atlantic states and the South. He also wrote numerous articles, authored the book *Spanish Details* (1924), and chaired the committee that produced *Great Georgian Houses of America* (1933–37), in which Virginia houses predominate. He married Harriet Townsend, an architectural writer from Lexington, Virginia, and formed many strong friendships in Richmond, including a bond with Herbert Clairborne, a principal in the construction firm of Clairborne and Taylor, who constructed the houses of the elite. Clairborne's wife was Virginia Christian, a holder of power in the women-only Garden Club of Virginia, and Bottomley received many of his commissions through the Clairbornes and the garden club.

Some of Bottomley's best-known works are sited along Monument Avenue in Richmond, where he designed an apartment house and seven single-family houses. Monument Avenue was laid out in 1890 as a memorial to the Confederacy and a site for homes for the wealthy. Although the depression of the 1890s and early 1900s hindered much housebuilding, statues were erected of Robert E. Lee (1890), Jeb Stuart and Jefferson Davis (1907), Stonewall Jackson (1919), and Matthew Fontaine Maury (1929). By the 1910s, the economy had recovered and Monument Avenue's elite status was commemorated in local author Ellen Glasgow's novel *Life and Gabriella* (1916): "Look at that house now, that's one of the finest in the city. Rushington built it—he made his money in fertilizer, and the one next with the green tiles belongs to Hanly, the tobacco trust fellow you know, and this whopper on the next square is where Albertson lives. He made his pile out of railroad stocks."[63]

Bottomley's first house on Monument Avenue, designed for Mr. and Mrs. H. Goslan and built between 1916 and 1918, does not follow Glasgow's parody. Rather, it indicates Bottomley's

William Lawrence Bottomley, H. L. Goslan House, Richmond, Virginia, 1916–18.

appeal to those who discriminated. Goslan, of Goslan & Nash, who specialized in real estate and investments, desired a reticent rather than bombastic house. Bottomley supplied a house that looked to the American colonial past but also acknowledged the English connection to Virginia.

Instead of the usual three- or five-bay treatment, Bottomley chose a four-bay facade with the entrance off center. With its tall front windows, the facade would not be out of place in a London or Boston square. The brick exterior is composed of an all-header bond, unlike the more common Flemish or American bonds, that gives it a subtle texture. This texture contrasts with a cast-stone pediment over the entrance. Such

richly carved pediments were comparatively unknown in the colonial period, and although Bottomley could have looked at Westover on the James River, the actual source probably comes from an English pattern book such as Belcher and Macartney's *Later Renaissance Architecture in England* (1901), or Field and Bunney's *English Domestic Architecture* (1905). The other exterior ornamental details specified were subtle quoins, a belt course, keystones over the tall windows, wrought-iron railings and balconies, and dentil blocks.

In a signature gesture of Bottomley's, the stairs do not greet the visitor; instead, a vestibule and hall leads one to the center of the house, where a spectacular, almost square two-story space contains an elaborate staircase and balcony. Ornamental detail is rich, with over-door pediments. The French-styled grisaille scenic wall, which is based on an 1831 woodblock print that was reproduced by A. L. Diament &

BELOW: Goslan House. Drawing room.

OPPOSITE: Goslan House. Stair hall.

Company, could have been selected by his wife, Harriet, who helped with the interiors. Bottomley liked to contrast spaces, both in shape, size, and axial alignment, so that they did not reveal themselves all at once. The large drawing room that stretched across the front contained appropriate wainscoting and paneling, but they were subdued so the focus could be on the elaborate fireplace mantel and chimney breast, with its adorning seascape painting selected by Mrs. Goslan. A shell motif appeared in the over-door pediments. Furniture was typically refined, including eighteenth-century English and Georgian pieces of reproduction, and perhaps a family heirloom. Glasgow did capture the spirit when she observed that "here and there, one might discover an authentic antique among all the varnished reproductions scattered to the far end of Monument Avenue . . . imponderable might be respected, but possessions were envied."[64]

The library was paneled in a dark gumwood. Over the fireplace hung a large map of Virginia. Bottomley's sister, Susan Meredith Bottomley, painted the map, which referenced the state's early origins in relation to Sir Walter Raleigh

Goslan House. Plan.

and Queen Elizabeth. Against this dark space, the sun room was light and contained a contemporary note with its Moravian-tiled floor. The dining room was appropriately spacious, articulated by twelve Roman Doric pilasters. A small walled garden with a fountain was at the rear.

JEFFERSON REVIVAL AND FISKE KIMBALL

Shack Mountain commands the landscape. Although diminutive in size in comparison to many other Colonial Revival homes, its large Tuscan columned portico draws the visitor in and provides a wide panorama of the Albemarle countryside and the Blue Ridge Mountains. A tour de force of design, the house is Fiske Kimball's homage to scholarship and to Thomas Jefferson.

In addition to his principal role in the writing of the Declaration of Independence in 1776, and his presidency from 1801 to 1809, Jefferson made important contributions to American architecture. Although not the first identifiable American architect, and sometimes criticized as "amateur" because of his lack of formal education in architecture, Jefferson's designs for the Virginia State House (1785–98; with C. L. Clerisseau), the University of Virginia (1814–26), several

Goslan House. Library.

Fiske Kimball, Shack Mountain, Charlottesville, Virginia, 1934–35.

of his own houses—including Monticello—and his contributions to Washington, D.C.'s plan and public buildings make him one of the great form-givers in American architecture. Strictly speaking, Jefferson's architecture does not fall in the colonial time period, since all of his surviving designs date from after independence. His architectural contributions were largely ignored, or, more properly, unknown during most of the nineteenth century. However, beginning in the 1890s, Jefferson emerged from obscurity to take center stage in the saga of American architecture, and also as a source for Colonial Revival.

The cooling of some of the passions of the Civil War—for Jefferson's stance on state's rights became one of the claims of secessionists—may have been one reason for Jefferson's emergence as a great form-giver. Also, his design of the University of Virginia was rediscovered and promoted as a prototype for institutions of higher learning. The fiery destruction of the Rotunda at the University in 1895, and the subsequent rebuilding by McKim, Mead & White, made Jefferson's accomplishments much better known to the public and the architectural community. During this period, books and arti-

cles begin to include his work, though controversy surrounded exactly what he designed. The 1913 publication by William A. Lambeth and Warren H. Manning of *Thomas Jefferson As an Architect and Designer of Landscape* put to rest some of the argument and had the distinction of being the first historical monograph devoted to an American architect.[65] Kimball's *Thomas Jefferson, Architect,* which—nearly a century later—remains one of the classics in architectural history, followed this volume in 1916.

Sidney Fiske Kimball came from an old Boston family and took an architecture degree at Harvard. Kimball completed his doctorate in architectural history on Jefferson's design for the Virginia State House while teaching at the University of Michigan. Meanwhile, the heirs of Thomas Jefferson Coolidge Jr., a descendant of Jefferson (and cousin of John Gardner Coolidge of the Stevens-Coolidge house), who had collected his papers and given them to the Massachusetts Historical Society, enlisted Kimball to study and write a book on Jefferson's architectural drawings. The large folio-sized volume, published in 1916, reproduced many of Jefferson's drawings and set new standards for the analysis and study of Jefferson's sources, as well as for assessing his accomplishments.

In 1919, Kimball moved to the University of Virginia to establish an architectural program and continued publishing. His *Domestic Architecture of the American Colonies and Early Republic* (1922) synthesized many years of research by him and others such as Ogden Codman Jr., who provided information and loaned him drawings. A diehard classicist, Kimball argued in *American Architecture* (1925) that Jefferson provided the breakthrough to a "new sense of form," or a "classical movement" in which "America was thus not merely a follower—rather, a leader."[66] Kimball's classical stance stood at one pole of the Colonial Revival debate of the interwar years; it celebrated the abstract and timeless features versus the equally treasured quaint and "olde-time" charm.

Kimball and his wife, Marie, who was also a scholar and wrote several books on Jefferson, left Charlottesville in 1923 for New York University; then, in 1925, he accepted the directorship at the Philadelphia Museum of Art. He remained there until 1955, amassing one of the great American collections of art from many continents. He still maintained an interest in architecture, going on to publish more books, such as *Mr. Samuel McIntire* (1940) and *Creation of the Rococo* (1943), in addition to writing many articles. He retained ties to Virginia by serving on the board of the Thomas Jefferson Memorial Foundation, which purchased Monticello in 1923, and he directed its restoration into the 1950s. Additionally, he served as head of the advisory board for the Colonial Williamsburg restoration and directed restoration work at Gunston Hall and Stratford Hall, the Robert E. Lee family's ancestral home. As a member of the board for the Thomas Jefferson Memorial in Washington, D.C., he picked John Russell Pope to design the great domed structure.

In May 1935, the Kimballs purchased land outside of Charlottesville as the location for a vacation retreat and retirement home. Kimball's design for the house was in many ways the embodiment of his architectural philosophy. Although he had designed several houses and other buildings early in his career, this building would be different—a place that he and Marie would live in, a summation of his research and thinking, and a statement of propriety. Consequently, it was Jeffersonian, but reinterpreted.

Originally, Kimball intended to call it Tusculum, after the Tuscan order, but the local name Shack Mountain, after the original landowners, the Shackelford family, stuck. The house was not grand; Kimball avoided one of Monticello's most distinguishing features, a dome, and instead focused the house around the portico and the two interconnected bow-ended rooms at the rear. The model Kimball had in mind was Jefferson's 1802 additions to Farmington, a house outside of Charlottesville, drawings of which Kimball had published.

Kimball drew from Jefferson's siting of houses, placing his own house on top of a hill with the drive positioned perpendicularly to the front through the woods, so the visitor might see both the house and the wider landscape. The Tuscan order, which Jefferson employed in front of the dormitory rooms on the Lawn at the University, was the lowest of the five ancient classical orders and usually appeared in common buildings. For his portico, Kimball chose the Tuscan and a very simple entablature. Instead of Jefferson's occasionally too-fussy additions of railings and ornamental details, Kimball kept Shack Mountain austere. A low wing to the rear of the front pavilion contained the bedrooms and service facilities and gave the house an additive note similar to Farmington. Only a simple cornice caps the rear section. The kitchen door is marked by a Chinese-style lattice railing.

The main entrance is on what appears to be the central axis, but it leads to a small quarter-round vestibule that redirects movement into the parlor. Through a wide doorway, the parlor opens into the dining room, and also has a corresponding quarter-round alcove that leads to the bedroom-service wing. Hence, the parlor is an octagon, a shape that Jefferson loved and used throughout his career. The interior entablature is full Tuscan, mimicking the exterior (as Jefferson would have done) while providing the rooms with a monumental aspect. All the interior moldings, as well as the parlor's fireplace, are Jeffersonian. The tall, triple-sash floor-to-ceiling windows are also Jeffersonian and articulate a concern with light and a connection to the outdoors. Similarly, the bow ends of each room project outwards. Also Jefferson-inspired is the flow of space between the rooms. Most of the furniture was designed—after late-eighteenth- and early-nineteenth-century models—to be in scale with the rooms. A medallion of Jefferson in profile hangs over the dining room doorway.

The Kimballs intended to properly landscape the house, but their busy schedules prevented any significant garden work. They visited the house most frequently during the Christmas season and the late spring. Kimball retired from the museum in 1955 intending to devote more time to the house, but he and Marie died within five months of each other later that year. The house was sold to friends who, while maintaining and enhancing Kimball's interpretation of Jefferson, cultivated a suitable terraced garden.

A SOUTHERN INTERPRETATION OF NEW ENGLAND

The Sandison House in the Buckhead section of Atlanta, Georgia, is an example of how styles associated with one par-

Philip Trammell Shutze, Dr. Calvin Sandison House, Atlanta, Georgia, 1938.

First Floor Plan

Sandison House. Plan.

Sandison House. Rear facade, with alterations.

ticular region could be imported and utilized elsewhere. Although architect Philip Trammell Shutze had a reputation for designing impressive mansions, when Dr. Sandison requested a house with few pretenses, Shutze accepted the challenge and suggested they visit New England. Shutze, who owned a huge collection of books, prepared Sandison for the trip with an examination of houses they might see. Their exact itinerary remains unclear, but it is known that they saw numerous houses in the Boston area, including the Fairbanks-Morse House in Dedham. Long known as the earliest surviving New England house, it was described by Robert Peabody in 1877 as possessing "picturesqueness," thanks in large part to its different roof forms. In 1881, it became the first colonial-era house to be published with photographs in the premier architectural journal of those years, *The American Architect*.[67]

The house that Shutze designed for the Sandisons departed from his usual mode of Italian Baroque or English Georgian. A member of the firm of Hentz, Adler & Shutze, he had tentatively experimented with a subdued Art Deco style in the early 1930s, but his real forte was the historical styles. Shutze was born in 1890 in Columbus, Georgia, to a prosperous family, and he studied architecture at Georgia Technical University. Georgia Tech was ruled by the Beaux Arts system that stressed the classical principles of design. He worked part time for his teachers Neel Reid and Hal Heinz, both of whom had studied at Columbia University and encouraged him to go north for another degree. After Columbia, Shutze again worked for Reid and Heinz and then won the prestigious Rome Prize, which gave him three years at the American Academy in Rome. Already a stickler for detail, Shutze had the opportunity in Rome to measure, draw,

and photograph the great classical monuments. He served in the American Red Cross during the war, traveled several times back and forth across the Atlantic, and worked briefly in New York before settling in Atlanta with his old employers. After Reid's death, Shutze became a partner and took charge of the firm's design. According to Shutze's biographer, Elizabeth Dowling, his associates claimed that "he designed everything the office produced."[68] The system was autocratic, with Shutze making the preliminary detailed and proportioned sketches, which were then worked up by his staff. Then Shutze would critique, revise, refine, and draft special details, though the staff prepared most of the working drawings. In the case of the Sandison House, the working drawings were signed by draftsman Ike Williamson, though Adler added some construction details.

For the Sandison House, Shutze may have made some measurements of the Fairbanks-Morse House while visiting there, but detailed drawings of it were available in many publications. Shutze basically followed the three-part form, roof shapes, and materials of the New England example but with a significant difference: he reversed the entrance and sited the house overlooking the river below. The entrance to the Sandison House is through what would be the kitchen addition at the rear of the Fairbanks-Morse House. A great long sloping roof rises up with the small hill on which the house is sited. On the other side, large windows and porches allow views of the gardens and river bottom and reveal that it is really a three-story house built into the hillside. The exterior shutters are a twentieth-century addition, as is the treatment of the porch elevation, which draws upon carriage sheds for its fenestration. Being a Depression-era house, the interiors were subdued. The plan had little connection with the Fairbanks-

TOP: Sandison House. Dining room.

BOTTOM: Sandison House. Living room.

Morse House, except for the large fireplace, which faintly echoes the original. The through-entrance hall was Southern, as was the porch overlooking the gardens and river. Furnishings have changed over the years but subdued reproductions have been the norm.

OHIO REVIVAL: BROMFIELD'S MALABAR FARM

Louis Bromfield, the Pulitzer prize–winning, bestselling novelist once posed the question, "Where exactly is Ohio?" His response was: "It is the farthest west of the east, and farthest east of the west, the farthest north of the south and the farthest south of the north, and it is probably the richest area of

its size in the world." Initially settled by Revolutionary War veterans who received land grants as payment for their time, Ohio's first white settlement was established in 1788. Admitted to the Union as the seventeenth state in 1803, Ohio was the first state carved out of the old Northwest Territory. In 1936, the early buildings were characterized architecturally by Ihna T. Frary: "If you are familiar with the early architecture of the thirteen original colonies or states, you can determine pretty accurately the origin of the early settlers in almost any old Ohio town by studying the character of the buildings which survive there, and comparing these with their eastern prototypes." Frary explained that Northern Ohio—sometimes known as the Western Reserve—contained settlers from New England and, consequently, the architecture resembled that region's, while Southern Ohio was settled by settlers from Virginia, Maryland, Pennsylvania, and farther south, which resulted in houses that reflected the sensibilities of the South. Frary, formerly a designer with the Brooks Household Art Company of Cleveland, and then with the Cleveland Museum of Art, had spent more than a decade traveling the state taking photographs and researching old houses, churches, and other public buildings. In common with his Eastern colleagues, Frary included the Greek, Roman, and other pre–Civil War revivals in his study. He was the Ohio expert and assisted the architect Louis Andre Lamoreux in the design of the "Big House" and other structures at Bromfield's model farm, Malabar, near Mansfield, Ohio.[69]

Bromfield was born in Mansfield in 1896. His family had, after the Civil War, lost a large farm in a mortgage foreclosure. His father sang the praises of country life, and Bromfield was raised with a Jeffersonian idealism of the virtues of the yeoman farmer and the agrarian tradition. At the urging of his strong-willed mother, Bromfield determined to be a writer and moved East to study. He served in the ambulance corps in France during World War I, became a journalist, married Mary Wood of New York, and wrote a novel, *The Green Bay Tree* (1924), which became a bestseller. Set in a fictionalized nineteenth-century version of Mansfield, the novel traced the passing of "the small private enterprise . . . succeeded by the day of the great corporation." His subsequent book, *Early Autumn* (1927), won the Pulitzer prize, and in 1929 he received the O'Henry Short Story Award. Touted as "the most promising of our young novelists," Bromfield and his wife moved to France, where he continued to write bestsellers and admire the attachment generations of French farmers had to their soil. His 1933 novel, *The Farm,* set in nineteenth-century Ohio, portrayed the loss of country life to industry. The conclusion is poignant and politically charged: "'Some day,' old Jamie had said, 'there will come a reckoning and the country

Louis Andre Lamoreux, Malabar Farm, Mansfield, Ohio, 1939–40. East facade.

will discover that farmers are more necessary than traveling salesmen, that no nation can exist or have any solidity which ignores the land. But it will cost the country dear.' "[70]

Bromfield's conservative political views, his dated style of storytelling, his increasing involvement with Hollywood, and his antipathy to modern experimental literature, alienated many critics and reviewers, but the public still loved his fiction. By 1938, the Bromfields, now with three daughters, sensed the war clouds gathering and decided to return to Mansfield. Bromfield intended to purchase a farm, and instead of mining the soil, as had earlier farmers, he would steward the land with environmentally correct practices.

A few miles south of Mansfield, Bromfield discovered the location, about which he wrote, "It was as if the Valley had been destined always to be a fiercely dominant part of my existence, especially on its spiritual and emotional side." He purchased several run-down farms totaling about 600 acres, rented more acreage, named the group Malabar, and set about making his dream come true. The name came from the Malabar Coast of India, which he had visited and used in his novels. Bromfield explained the choice: "India made the farm possible."[71] A large man with a dominant personality who was used to getting his way, Bromfield established control of the farm, which became very much his affair. To support it, he continued to write for the movies, produce novels, and explain his farming experiment in several books such as *Pleasant Valley* (1945), *Malabar Farm* (1948), and *From My Experience* (1955).[72]

Such a dream needed a manor, or a "Big House," and an architect to design what he referred to as an "apotheosis of Ohio architecture." Bromfield, who remained intimately involved in the design processs, described Louis Andre Lamoreux as "a Mansfield architect of good taste, who knew his Ohio countryside and his Ohio architecture." Lamoreux, who had graduated from Cornell, described his meeting with Bromfield in January 1939: "If I ever had any compunctions about Friday the 13th, I lost them after that day . . . little did I dream of the experiences, the out and out fun, and the constant and consistently changing series of events. . . . Mr. Bromfield wanted a good unostentatious farmhouse in the Ohio tradition, yet no tradition existed for it." Bromfield determined they would retain and incorporate the old Herring farmhouse on the property, which he called "a plain square, uncompromising house without architectural detail but possessing the beauty of an honest, functional house." To him, it represented "the line of continuity and tradition." Lamoreux later recalled spending many "dreary months of the Depression with the Ohio office of the Historic Ameri-

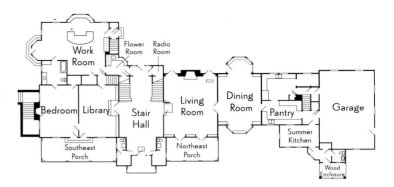

Malabar Farm. Plan.

can Building Survey, and to my knowledge there just was not an existing example of Western Reserve architecture of the scale of the Herring house."

Bromfield desired a house "which after a year or two looked as if it belongs there on that hillside shelf in the middle of the rich Ohio country." Bromfield wanted the " new additions . . . to be built at different levels, with slightly varying style so that they would give the impression of having been added from time to time over a period of a hundred years or more." As Lamoreux recalled it, they were "creating an assembled house, parts of this and that from several periods, and above all, its entirety must be in good scale and taste." As to style, Bromfield later explained that "because the Greek revival style of Thomas Jefferson had left a great imprint on all early houses in Ohio, I want that style to dominate both the outside and inside." He also noted that he had brought many furnishings and paintings back from France and they "fitted into the frame of the classical Greek revival style." He acknowledged the impact New England had on the design, and resolved that, since Malabar lay right on the border between North and South, the house should reflect the sensibilities of both areas.[73]

Lamoreux and Bromfield turned to Frary, who had recently published his book, for help, and they poured over photographs and took to the road looking for sources. Frary directed them to the Dr. Peter Allen House, located in the Western Reserve town of Kinsman. Built around 1821, the Allen House had been designed with English and American pattern books to create the delicate pilasters, frieze, and window details. For the two porches that fronted the wings, the builder chose cast-iron pillars with grapes and leaves resembling those of a house from the Ohio River town of Marietta.

OVERLEAF: Malabar Farm. South facade.

Frary also provided photos and information on houses not pictured in his book, such as the lunette for the east gable from a Twinsburg house. The garage gable came from a house in Richfield, and the entrance trellis was borrowed from an 1835 house in Lakewood. The Taft-Sinton House in Cincinnati, the Matthews House in Painesville, and several Norwalk houses provided trim, window and door surrounds, and cornice details. Houses in Kirkland inspired details for the door area, and Bromfield speculated that they came from work that Brigham Young had done during his carpentering days in that town.[74] Fragments of Ohio houses found a resting place at Malabar, such as the material for the front door, which came from a Chagrin Falls house destroyed by fire.

The overall proportions of the original farmhouse, which took up the front southeast wing, controlled the additions. It was gutted, and to its rear, or west, a large wing was added. On the north side of the old Herring House was placed the new main entrance wing, which contained a great stair hall. To this was added a long wing with porches, bays, and smaller wings. The house appeared to flow along the hillside. The original sandstone foundation was retained, while a standing-seam tin roof replaced what had been slate. From a small frame house, it had grown into a structure containing thirty-two rooms with seven bedrooms and five baths. Throughout the process, Bromfield remained involved, offering advice and frequently demanding changes and last-minute alterations.

For the interior, Lamoreux copied moldings from early Ohio buildings and specified black walnut doors, which had been common. The wide entrance hall was dominated by twin staircases and a landing. Niches on the landing were intended to contain copies of Houdon's busts of Lafayette and Jefferson, reflecting the family's strong connections with France and Bromfield's admiration of Jefferson's agrarian philosophy.[75] Beyond this area, different tastes became apparent. The living room/salon had an American eagle over the fireplace and some antiques, but the mirrored wall and marble fire surrounds were more cosmopolitan and contemporary.

Malabar Farm. Porch.

Malabar Farm. East facade (service wing).

Bromfield's quarters took up the entire ground floor plus the additions that had been made to the old Herring House. He had a library, his own bedroom, and a large workroom with a massive desk containing twenty-nine drawers. Here he would write and entertain with his boxer dogs lying about. Above his study, on the second floor, his agent and secretary, George Hawkins, had a room that was connected to his by back stairs. Hawkins deplored what he called the "humus, mucus, retch and vetch" of farming, and his room resembled a suite at the St. Regis Hotel in New York.[76] Mary Bromfield, who always bowed to her husband's enthusiasms, had her bedroom on the second floor, while the three daughters were off in a wing, where there were also several guest rooms. Garden terraces and porches opened off many of the downstairs rooms, and flowerbeds predominated.

A significant part of the Malabar dream had to do with the farm, and adjacent to the house Bromfield remodeled and constructed a complex of barns and other structures such as a chicken house, greenhouse, and silo. The design of these buildings is attributed to Bromfield, Lamoreux, and various farm managers who looked to earlier Ohio buildings and to modern and efficient farming practices for design ideas. Bromfield wanted to restore the worn-out soil by proper scientific methods and prove that a living could be earned

ABOVE: Malabar Farm. Stair hall.

BELOW: Malabar Farm. Stair hall.

OPPOSITE, TOP: Malabar Farm. Living room.

OPPOSITE, BOTTOM: Malabar Farm. Sitting room.

Malabar Farm. Dining room.

from a "family farm" that was properly managed. He styled himself as "the boss" and envisioned the farm becoming self-sufficient, growing most of its own food. He also set up a cooperative plan whereby farmers could work for him and, in return, receive room and board. Bromfield would ensure financial support until the farm turned a profit. The Malabar farm employed contour plowing, strip and crop rotation, soil enrichment, and other environmentally correct practices. Bromfield also envisioned an educational mission and invited tourists, farmers, and agricultural students to Malabar. At its peak, during the mid-1940s, he was feeding forty farmers and students a day. In spite of his idealism, however, Bromfield came to realize that a self-sufficient farm did not make sense, and in the post–World War II years Malabar increasingly became a pasturing farm known for its specialty grasses, legumes, dairy herd, and cattle.

Bromfield's exuberant personality brought celebrities to the many guest rooms at Malabar. James Cagney showed up to run the roadside produce stand, and Joan Fontaine assisted with a calf's birth. Humphrey Bogart and Lauren Bacall married and spent a portion of their honeymoon in the Big House. Bromfield delighted in running the place, traveling the fields in his jeep surrounded by his cadre of Boxer dogs.

In a sense, Malabar represents fiction turned into reality. But the reality of self-sufficient farming proved elusive, as did the Big House as an emblem of family cheer. The farm never made a profit, and Bromfield had to support it with his magazine writing, novels, and Hollywood screenplays. Eventually he became debt-ridden, but his concern with being "the boss" made it impossible for him to turn the house over to his daughters. They were alienated, and two years after his death, in 1956, his daughters sold the farm to a nonprofit organiza-

tion, which also found the house difficult to maintain. In 1972, the state of Ohio took over the farm and buildings and today runs it as a state park and demonstration farm.

COLONIAL WILLIAMSBURG: THE GREAT TASTEMAKER

By 1937, the full intent of the restoration of Williamsburg had become apparent. Work began in 1928, and on September 26, 1932, a formal dedication took place with the completion of the reconstructed Raleigh Tavern. To most Americans, Colonial Williamsburg had until this point existed as a concept rather than a physical reality. With the 1936 reconstruction and opening of the Capitol and the Governor's Palace, and the substantial completion of Duke of Gloucester Street, the public could now physically walk into the eighteenth century and sit and hear the words of Patrick Henry and other Revolutionary War heroes. John D. Rockefeller Jr., who funded most of Colonial Williamsburg, wrote that the project "offered an opportunity to restore a complete area and free it entirely from alien or inharmonious surroundings as well as to preserve the beauty and charm of the old building and gardens." He went on to observe, "As the work has progressed I have come to feel that perhaps an even greater value is the lesson that it teaches of patriotism, high purpose, and unselfish devotion of our forefathers to the common good."[77]

Rockefeller's remarks interpret Colonial Williamsburg as an instrument for teaching patriotism. But reconstructed Williamsburg was also a great marketing tool that demonstrated how Americans might live if they so choose. Laid out on a grid, the town was hierarchical, with nodal points dominated by public buildings: the Capitol, the Governor's Palace, Bruton Parish Church, and the Wren Building of the College of William and Mary. Commerce appeared in two areas along Duke of Gloucester Street: the historical section near the Capitol, and then a new shopping area, Merchants Square, near the college, which was mistaken by many as authentic, but in fact was designed to look old. Neat houses and gardens dominated the tree-lined streets of the town. In the company of the costumed guides and interpreters, visitors were encouraged to step back in time.

The story of the restoration of Colonial Williamsburg has its share of complexities and, indeed, surprises. Founded in 1699 as the colonial capital of Virginia (the successor to Jamestown), Williamsburg witnessed many important events connected with the Revolution. Replaced by Richmond as the state capital in 1779, many—though not all—of

Perry, Shaw & Hepburn, Governor's Palace, Colonial Williamsburg, Virginia,
1932–36. Detail of entrance hall ceiling.

its colonial-era buildings survived into the early-twentieth century. The Reverend (and Doctor) William A. R. Goodwin, who served from 1903 to 1907 as rector of Bruton Parish Church (a building that dates to 1711–15) and oversaw its restoration, returned to the College of William and Mary in 1923 as a professor of Bible studies and director of the college's endowment. Within a few years, he again took the pastorate of Bruton Parish. Goodwin conceived the idea of restoring the town to its colonial splendor and cast about for a financial angel. He struck pay dirt in 1924 at a Phi Beta Kappa dinner in New York City, where he met John D. Rockefeller Jr., the son of the founder of Standard Oil Company and one of the world's richest individuals. Rockefeller was already involved with significant restoration projects at Versailles, Fontainebleau, Rheims, Athens, and elsewhere.

Rockefeller visited in 1926 and, as Goodwin described, "confidentially authorized the preparation of preliminary drawings to help visualize the possibilities of the dream of a Williamsburg restoration." Goodwin later claimed (rather disingenuously), "No further commitments of any kind were made or suggested at that time." Events then moved very quickly; the Boston-based Colonial Revival firm of Perry, Shaw & Hepburn were hired, and research was carried out with, as Goodwin described, "complete secrecy," including nighttime reconnaissance missions. A private meeting with Rockefeller and his aides took place in a hotel in New York in late 1927, and shortly thereafter "authority was given to proceed with the purchase of property." Considerable property was purchased before the public announcement in June 1928 that a major restoration/reconstruction would take place.[78]

The work carried out in the next several years was impressive: archives were scoured in Europe and America; an early print at the Bodleian Library in Oxford, England, provided several views of major public buildings; extensive archaeology turned up materials and original garden layouts and plants; colonial brickmaking was rediscovered; paint scraping yielded a new paint palette for the period; and interiors and furnishings received a new examination. By 1937, in addition to the restoration/reconstruction of three colonial-era buildings at the College of William and Mary, sixty-seven other buildings had been restored, ninety-one buildings were reconstructed, eighteen modern buildings had been removed from the historical area, and 459 modern buildings demolished. An advisory committee headed by Fiske Kimball provided guidance, and a generation of architects, restorers, and historians were trained.

By most measures, the standards for restoration at Williamsburg were very high, but some liberties were taken. The boxwood maze behind the Governor's Palace came from

OVERLEAF: Governor's Palace. Garden facade.

Governor's Palace. Ballroom.

the fertile imagination of landscape architect Arthur A. Shurcliff, assisted by some minor topographical sources. Other gardens were enhanced, as the restorers consciously refused to accept that colonial gardens were rather bare, simple, and functional. Instead of brick pathways, they would have contained broken crockery, oyster shells, and chicken bones.[79] During the colonial period, most of the outbuildings would have remained unpainted. At Colonial Williamsburg, the houses were over-furnished and filled with top-of-the-line items that were far beyond the economic level of many of the original owners. African-Americans were portrayed in subservient roles, but the quality of their lifestyle was generally ignored. Later reinterpretations have changed and corrected certain aspects of Colonial Williamsburg and added nuances. But the main theme remains: Colonial Williamsburg illumi-

OPPOSITE: Governor's Palace. Entrance hall.

nates how the heroic generation of patriots lived on the eve of the Revolution.

Colonial Williamsburg contained other lessons as well. It became a paradigm of the twentieth-century garden suburb with its generous open space, its heavy vegetation and trees (some experts believe there are at least 40 percent more than during the 1770s), its overall cleanliness, its concealment of modern utilities, and its neat reproductions of historical buildings. The homemakers' press fell over itself praising the restoration and seeking lessons from its success. A writer for *Better Homes & Gardens* felt it offered "an example of one way by which urban communities can be made ideal places in which to live."[80]

For most of the public, the line between restored buildings and those that had been reconstructed was imperceptible. The Governor's Palace, destroyed by fire in 1781, was a reconstruction. The original was among the largest buildings in pre-Revolutionary America. Its dominant five-bayed facade and flankers to the front, its rich staircase, and the large ballroom to the rear, became a model of refined living

Governor's Palace. Dining room.

with innumerable imitations. Many houses were reconstructed, while others got major restorations. The Peyton Randolph house began as two small houses on adjoining lots, which were joined about the middle of the eighteenth century by a large central section. In the nineteenth century, one of the original wings was removed and an elaborate two-story "Carpenter's Gothic" front porch was added. It was restored in the late 1930s and the lost wing was reconstructed. One of the reasons for its importance was the fine interior paneling of yellow pine, with walnut doors, window sash, and trim. Similar stories could be told of other Williamsburg houses.

The houses of Williamsburg provided a new repertory of plans, and the foundation set up a reproduction arm that produced authorized copies of furniture, paint, fabrics, wallpaper, and other items for sale. By the mid-1930s, most of the architectural press in the United States had converted to modernism, hence *Architectural Record*'s reference to Colonial Williamsburg as a "restoration" with little relevance to con-

temporary design.[81] The homemakers' press saw it differently, as did the architects in charge, Perry, Shaw & Hepburn, who provided model house designs to *House and Garden,* which sold the plans. A writer for the magazine praised the plans as "our future home designs. . . . We come to Williamsburg then, not merely to admire but also to study and learn."[82] The number of plans the American public purchased (and subsequently built) remains unknown, but imitations of the houses at Colonial Williamsburg became a staple of American single-family housing for the next sixty-plus years.

Colonial Williamsburg seemed to offer respite from the complex problems that dominated the 1930s. A writer in 1938 saw it as an antidote to the Great Depression and "these topsy-turvy times," claiming that it restored "faith in democracy."[83] Although the architectural press held Williamsburg at arm's length, the professional architectural community hailed it. The AIA held their annual convention there in 1936. A writer for *Better Homes and Gardens* observed: "Williamsburg isn't only attracting tourists this summer by its historical appeal; it also is stimulating the desire for better homes."[84]

Governor's Palace. Bedroom.

Colonial Williamsburg offered a template, or as *House and Garden*'s editor, Richardson Wright, pronounced in 1937, "the future can learn from the past . . . the spirit of ancient Williamsburg and the actuality of its splendid buildings and homes now restored have a definite, necessary and vital message for your times."[85] Similarly, in the 1980s, when modernism in architecture came under scrutiny along with suburban sprawl, Williamsburg's idealized past became, according to architect Robert A. M. Stern, "eminently usable." Citing Colonial Williamsburg's motto, "That the Future may learn from the Past," Stern suggested that the grid plan, the absence of the automobile, and the carefully

restored and re-created buildings were an object lesson for Americans and a "textbook for the future."[86]

The power of Colonial Williamsburg can scarcely be underestimated; it is a place that nearly every American has heard about and many have visited. It contains 88 original eighteenth-century buildings and more than 400 reconstructed structures on 301 acres. More than 100 million people have visited and its yearly attendance (paid) is about 750,000, in addition to the approximately two million more that just walk down Duke of Gloucester Street, where access is free.[87] Later imitators such as Disneyland have attracted more visitors but, as a model of how Americans might live, Williamsburg apotheosized Colonial Revival and made it permanent.

Endurance

WORLD WAR II TO THE PRESENT

Most treatments of American art and architecture since World War II emphasize the triumph of modernism and the vanquishing of historicism, especially the Colonial Revival. Artists adopted abstract idioms in painting and sculpture, and for the serious composer, atonal or repetitive rhythmic music became the approved method. Glass-walled and concrete buildings transformed cities and the countryside. Molded-plywood furniture by Charles and Ray Eames achieved iconic status, and museums exhibited houses with flat roofs, exposed-steel walls, and minimal furnishings. By the mid-1950s, most American architectural education had come under the modernist hegemony, and students who desired to design in colonial or other historical idioms were told to go elsewhere, though elsewhere seldom existed.

A lack of documentation and perspective make the recording of the recent history of Colonial Revival a tenuous task. One looks in vain for an article on a Colonial Revival house in the professional architectural magazine of today. But in spite of the many critics ignoring and condemning Colonial Revival, the idiom has survived, as a drive through almost any suburb will show. American suburbia is "Colonial Revival–Land." The quality of these structures varies, but present in the landscape will be Cape Cod cottages along with three- and five-bay brick and/or clapboarded Georgian-derived houses. Certainly, great houses in the various modern idioms have been constructed between 1945

Anne Fairfax and Richard Sammons, Farmlands, Cooperstown, New York, 2002.

and today, but during this same period Colonial Revival remained the architectural image of choice of many Americans.

PUBLICATIONS

An aspect of the conversion to modernism and the dismissal of historicism and Colonial Revival lay with the new role of the historian as the prophet of the modern. Most architectural historians were architects who needed to be conversant with the past, although exceptions existed, such as John Ruskin and Montgomery Schuyler, who were writers and critics but not architects. The role of earlier architects such as Charles McKim, and historian/architects such as Fiske Kimball and Joseph Everett Chandler, have been noted; they researched, published, and pleaded for a particular view of the past. But this changed as the professional architectural historian emerged. Individuals such as Henry-Russell Hitchcock and Lewis Mumford played seminal roles as they merged the functions of critic and historian. They argued that buildings should reflect their time, and, since the twentieth century seemed to typify new building processes, materials, and a changed intellectual climate, it followed that architecture should do the same. This canard that buildings should reflect their age derived from the Hegelian concept of *zeitgeist,* or "spirit of the age," meaning that the architect (or artist or designer) in contact with such spirit would create new forms, styles, and languages. The possibility that defining the zeitgeist could be a tricky operation, or that several zeitgeists might exist, never seemed to concern modernism's proponents. Rather, this new approach captured the professional architectural magazines, and institutions like the Museum of Modern Art in New York sprang up to support it.

Henry-Russell Hitchcock came from an old New England family. He taught at several universities and had an extensive writing career between the late 1920s and the 1980s. The principal author and creator of the International Style exhibit and accompanying books for the Museum of Modern Art, Hitchcock introduced Americans to European modernism. According to Hitchcock, the past and the historical styles should be replaced by the new, or, as he lamented in a 1939 catalog entry on McKim, Mead & White's H. A. C. Taylor House: "The inertia of the Colonial Revival . . . has retarded for a generation the development of modern architecture in the Eastern United States, and retards it still today." Although Hitchcock could appreciate historical figures such as H. H. Richardson, in his hands Richardson became a predecessor of modernism. By 1952, Hitchcock rejoiced with triumph: "Modernism had arrived . . . it is suc-

cessful . . . what used to be called 'traditional' architecture is dead if not buried."[1]

Hitchcock is but one example of the American historian/critic who championed modernism. Another contributing factor was America's inferiority complex vis-à-vis European art and architecture: Americans copied too much and needed a new, modern voice. The roles played by European historians and critics—such as Sigfried Giedion and Nikolaus Pevsner—in defining American modernism was significant.[2] If the United States wanted to rival Europe artistically, then it needed to adopt modernism.

Although major books on Early American architecture were published, no historian would dare assert these works as models for contemporary practice.[3] The major exception was Haywood and Blanche Cirker of the Dover Publishing Company, who made a career of republishing paperback editions of early pattern books and architectural histories, many of which contained colonial and Colonial Revival topics.

Architectural history did expand its coverage, and aspects of Colonial Revival received selected study. Vincent Scully's *The Shingle Style* (1955) treated the shingled incarnation, McKim, Mead & White's Isaac Bell House especially, as part of a search for a genuine American architecture. According to Scully, the downfall came with McKim, Mead & White's Colonial Revival conversion: "The [H. A. C.] Taylor House and its descendants made antiquarianism respectable and originality suspect."[4] By the 1970s, the forces that led to postmodernism in architecture began to direct scholars toward the study of Victorian, Beaux Arts, and the Colonial Revival. However, they treated them as movements located in the past, with little validity for the present day. The Colonial Revival engendered deep suspicion, or as one scholar wrote, introducing a collection of papers presented at a symposium, "My judgment is that while a little colonial revival may be a good thing, a great deal of it is a sign of personal or group disorder."[5]

In the late 1970s and 1980s, a shift in view developed among a few historians and architects. Scully revised his earlier dismissal of Colonial Revival, and acknowledged the problems of modernism; he argued for a "new urbanist" approach. In a *New York Times* article, Scully praised the New Urbanists for their "revival of the vernacular and classical traditions and their reintegration into the mainstream of modern architecture in its fundamental aspect: the structure of communities, the building of towns." A few architects, most notably Robert A. M. Stern and Allan Greenberg, also worked as historians, researching and writing books on the history of architecture that reflected their life as designers.[6]

The roles of architectural magazines and professional architectural historians only tells part of the story, for at another level—one typically sneered at by the modernist architect and critic—there existed the homemaker and builder magazines and pattern books, which never abandoned Colonial Revival as the American style of choice. Magazines such as *American Home, House and Home,* and others publicized plans for Colonial Revival designs by architects such as Royal Barry Wills. Commercial house-plan factories ran a thriving business of selling blueprints and specifications by mail to prospective homeowners and builders. *The Essential Guide to Early American Home Plans* (1987) contained more than 330 homes, which included—among the twenty-eight varieties—"Cape Cod," "Georgian Elegance from the Past," and "Southern Colonial."[7]

A new class of specialized magazines aimed at the homeowner and architectural buff also emerged at this time. In the 1970s, *Architectural Digest,* which was founded in 1925, came under the editorial direction of Paige Rense, who shifted its editorial emphasis toward high-end interiors and homes. *Architectural Digest* published houses and interiors of all styles—modern, contemporary, revival, and historical; if an architect or interior designer wanted to gain a name, appearing in *Architectural Digest* trumped any professional publication. Imitators sprang up, such as *Southern Living* and *Southern Accents,* which, because of the demographics of their readership, emphasized the Colonial Revival–style house. Magazines such as *Old-House Journal, Old-House Interiors, Early-American Life, Victorian Homes, Victorian Interiors, Colonial Homes* (later renamed *Classic American Homes*), *Country Living,* and *American Bungalow* were more directed at the architecture enthusiast and historic preservationist. Obviously, these magazines catered to a variety of interests, but elements of Colonial Revival appeared even in those devoted to the Arts and Crafts movement.

HISTORIC PRESERVATION

The historic preservation movement grew in power and influence during the post–World War II years. Although earlier architects such as McKim and Chandler were preservationists, most modern-era architects spurned it as being peopled by pedagogues and antiquarians concerned exclusively with the homes of the wealthy. Although this elitist charge had some validity, in actuality vernacular structures received considerable attention in the *White Pine Series* and the Historic American Building Survey (HABS). HABS, founded in 1933 as part of the New Deal program to employ

out-of-work architects and historians, was rejuvenated in the 1950s and became a great sourcebook for Colonial Revivalist architects. Detailed drawings and photographs of Early American buildings provided a treasure trove of material for architects with a historical bent.

The continuing destruction of older buildings led to the foundation of the National Trust for Historic Preservation in 1949 and the creation of countless numbers of state and local historical- and preservation-minded organizations. The outcry over the 1963 destruction of McKim, Mead & White's Pennsylvania Station in New York helped raise this level of consciousness. Many cities and counties, primarily on the East Coast, added professional preservationists to their civic staffs and adopted ordinances to protect historic buildings. University-level programs concerned with architectural history and historic preservation came into being at the University of Virginia in the late 1950s, and at Columbia and Cornell in the 1960s. By the 1990s, nearly fifty such academic programs existed in the United States. The growth in educational programs was sparked by Congress's passage in 1966 of the Historic Preservation Act, which mandated a state-by-state survey of all buildings and objects of historical, cultural, and architectural significance, and the placement of important examples on the National Register. The federal government, largely through the National Park Service, accepted a much larger role in the preservation of its own properties and in assisting states and localities with such efforts.

One outcome of this increase in historic preservation activity was a change in our concept of history. Suddenly, the notion of what was historic had been vastly expanded, and it triggered a reconsideration of the context of buildings. Of new interest were vernacular buildings along with Victorian and early-twentieth-century structures. Even detested modern structures might be considered historic, assuming they met the fifty-year rule, as did Walter Gropius's own house at Lincoln, Massachusetts, and Philip Johnson's Glass House at New Canaan, Connecticut, both of which received designation.

But according validity to Colonial Revival took some time, as its genuineness remained suspect. Buildings such as McKim, Mead & White's Bell House gained approval, but structures that had been "Colonialized" were still considered false, since the government's standards for historic preservation condemned alterations that sought to create an earlier appearance. Government regulations stipulated that additions to older buildings had to be in a contemporary style, not a historical one. As noted in the discussion of the Hamilton House in South Berwick, Maine, SPNEA—when it took control of the house in 1949—set about removing the Colonial

Revival additions, returning the house to its late-eighteenth-century look. However, beginning in the 1980s, SPNEA changed direction and began to respect the Colonial Revival features. By 1995, governmental policy had been revised: "Changes to a property that have acquired historic significance in their own right will be retained and preserved."[8] Although Colonial Revival remained suspect among many historians and preservationists, the so-called failure of modernism challenged some of that thinking.

POSTMODERNISM

Cracks in the facade of modernism's success began to show in the 1960s and 1970s, only a few years after its proclaimed victory. A spate of books with titles such as *Complexity and Contradiction in Architecture, The Failure of Modern Architecture, The Death and Life of Great American Cities,* and *Form Follows Fiasco: Why Modern Architecture Hasn't Worked* appeared along with similarly titled articles in the professional and popular press.[9] Many differences existed between these critiques but several themes stood out: the inhumanness of modernism, the destruction of older downtowns, and the continuing loss of significant historical structures. This severe reaction to modernism, in some cases by its most prominent spokespersons—including Philip Johnson and Peter Blake—found a parallel with European architects such as James Stirling, Aldo Rossi, and Leon Krier.

The resulting "postmodernism," as it came to be called, contained a number of different thrusts. As a label, postmodern was applied to a wide variety of the arts—from literature to painting, to music, and architecture—though its interpretation differed widely depending on the art form. One element of postmodernism was a theoretical approach, which took au curant writings on epistemology, linguistics, reception, and critical theory and applied it to architecture and the other arts. Architecturally, the argument went that the modernist emphasis on function and structure lacked intellectual credibility and a new theoretical basis was needed. A Babel of tongues emerged that adopted the latest intellectual fads, such as deconstructivism. Another approach called for incorporating historical elements into contemporary architecture in a new way. Often concerned with continuity and the environment, whether urban or rural, this approach ranged from the occasionally cartoonish designs of Robert Venturi, Denise Scott-Brown, and others, to a more straightforward

Royal Barry Wills, "Good Cape Cod Houses Are Like This," ca. 1946.

juxtaposition of new and old, as with Hugh Newell Jacobsen. A new group of architects who looked to historical models as sources for contemporary design eventually grew out of this motifs-and-details approach. Among them were Robert A. M. Stern, Hartman and Cox, Alvin Holm, John Blateau, Allan Greenberg, Jaquelin Robertson, and Fairfax and Sammons.

The New Urbanism movement emerged from the heat of postmodernism and, by the 1990s, became a favorite of many developers. Spearheaded by architects Andres Duany and Elizabeth Plater-Zyberk of Florida, the New Urbanists preached density, traditional town plans, streets and communities that would be walkable, and traditional house styles. A regional ethos also governed some of the New Urbanist developments, hence Charleston-styled houses were more common in the South, whereas Georgian appeared in the North.

CONTINUATIONS

Although modernism dominated, architects specializing in historical design, and especially Colonial Revival, never entirely disappeared. For the most part, architects who had been educated as Colonial Revivalists during the 1920s and 1930s continued to design in the post–World War II years; a few changed with the times, but many kept on doing what they knew best. Most of these architects existed at the regional level, such as the Georgian classicist group of Philip Trammell Shutze, Jimmy Means, and others. At times they caught the national limelight, as with the Atlanta designer Edward Vason Jones, who, working in the Georgian and Federal styles, designed the Diplomatic Reception Rooms at the Department of State, and also several rooms at the White House in Washington, D.C. In spite of modernism's intrusion on the American campus, Colonial Revival persisted at several educational institutions, including Wake Forest University in Winston-Salem, North Carolina, which Jens Fred Larsen designed in the 1950s.[10]

Assisting in this historical recall were older museums—such as Colonial Williamsburg, which continued to build—and new museums such as Old Sturbridge Village, Historic Deerfield, and Winterthur. Henry Francis du Pont (1880–1969) began to form his collections in the 1920s, assisted by Henry Sleeper and others, but it was the opening of his massive and legendary house to the public in 1951 that put Winterthur on the map. Containing many priceless original objects and some original paneling, Winterthur really is Colonial Revival.[11]

Another important influence in historical recall were organizations such as the Classical America Society, founded in 1958 and led for many years by Henry Hope Read, who published a spirited defense of traditional design and a critique of modernism in *The Golden City* (1959). The Classical America Society never took advantage of the postmodern backlash; an alternative organization, the Institute of Classical Architecture, was founded in 1992 and, in time, subsumed the older organization. Most architectural education programs remained resolutely modern, though in the 1980s a few schools did experiment with traditional design. The University of Notre Dame became the most prominent institution to attempt a return to classicism. Beyond the university, efforts to train in the traditional styles came from groups such as Classical America and the Institute of Classical Design, and the Prince of Wales summer school.

HOUSES FOR GOOD LIVING: ROYAL BARRY WILLS

The most popular architect among the American middle class after World War II employed three names—and it was not Frank Lloyd Wright but Royal Barry Wills. *Life* magazine in 1946 anointed Wills as creating "the kind of house most Americans want," because his books sold more than 520,000 copies, and he had designed some 1,100 houses. Earlier, in 1938, Wills had dueled with Wright in a *Life* magazine contest over houses for the middle class. Wright entered one of his Usonian designs and Wills showed a Cape Cod house. Although the family initially favored Wright, they selected Wills in the end and built his Cape Cod design.[12]

Houses designed or influenced by Royal Barry Wills were ubiquitous, as Americans devoured his books, discovered his designs in homemaker and housebuilding magazines and newspapers, and either bought his plans or contacted him for a custom design. By the time of his death, in 1962, Wills and his firm were responsible for more than 2,500 houses. Wills was so popular that a writer for the *Saturday Evening Post* in 1958 observed: "Many a would-be home owner, surveying the infinite variations of Mr. Wills's Cape Codders in plan books and magazines has concluded that he is the man who somehow invented the design."[13]

Wills was born in the Boston suburb of Melrose in 1895 and he died in Boston in 1962. He studied architecture at the Massachusetts Institute of Technology, from which he graduated in 1918, and worked as a design engineer for the Turner Construction Company while moonlighting as an architect. In 1925 Wills opened a Boston architectural office and designed in the various historical idioms. With the onset of the Great Depression, he increasingly turned his attention to small (1,000 square feet) houses and began publishing a variety of colonial-derived designs with the Cape Cod idiom predominating. The prominent modernist Hugh Stubbins worked for Wills from 1935 to 1937, producing some International Style houses for the firm. However, Wills's reputation lay with the Colonial Revival house, and after World War II he was everywhere—constantly published, reviewed, and lauded, though always by the homemaker magazines, not the professional ones. Of course the modern architectural establishment did not care for Wills, but he never suffered because of it, and he often poked fun at his detractors with cartoons. Wills's sense of humor led him to write an article entitled "Confessions of a Cape Codder"(1949) , and the book *Houses Have Funny Bones* (1951). An astute businessman and an architect who understood his clients, he recognized what many Americans desired in a house and provided solutions.[14]

The house for Rudolph J. Schaeffer at Mamaroneck, New York, built in 1956, exemplifies Wills's mature handling of the Cape Cod cottage. The low-rising clapboarded house spreads across the lot through a series of additive wings. Heavy stone chimneys anchor the house. Wills paid attention to landscaping, maintaining several large trees on the site; the clustering of low azaleas along the house's foundation reflects twentieth-century suburban design, not eighteenth-century. A cobblestone driveway added an air of age to the necessary garage, which was disguised as a carriage shed. The entrance porch was unorthodox in the sense that colonial Capes seldom had such a feature, but Wills enhanced it with massive timbers and braces (sometimes called gunstocks) that might have come from a barn or outbuilding. Window sashes with twelve-over-twelve lights were employed on the main block. The plan owes a debt to eighteenth-century New England houses, but Wills made it more spacious and reconfigured some of the rooms. A wing off the rear contains a study and a screened porch. The entry hall has the traditional staircase

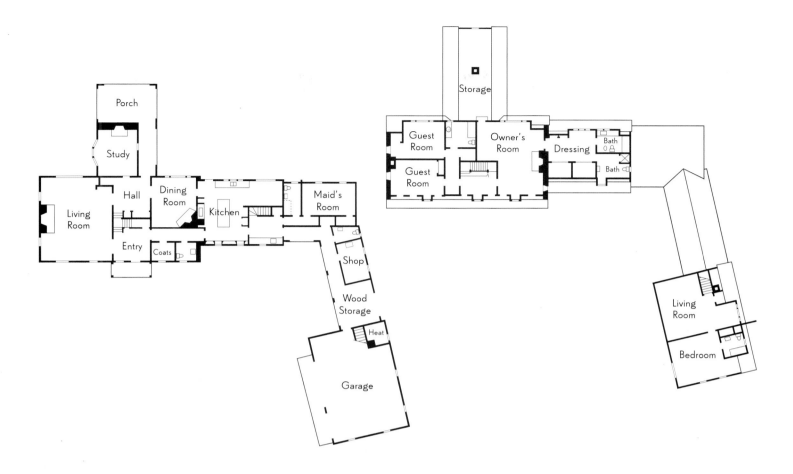

OPPOSITE: Royal Barry Wills, Rudolph J. Schaeffer House, Mamaroneck, New York, 1956.

ABOVE, TOP: Schaeffer House. Plans.

ABOVE, LEFT: Schaeffer House. Study.

RIGHT: Schaeffer House. Entrance hall.

with turned balusters—situated to greet the visitor—along with exposed beams and old square bricks for the floor, which are large to make for easier communication with the other rooms. The major rooms received appropriate detailing such as old-board wainscoting, or the more sophisticated dadoes and pilasters as seen in the dining room. Furnishings throughout were either antique or reproductions, which Wills advised on if asked.

Wills and his firm designed many houses in other Colonial Revival idioms, an example of which is the Walter Barker House (ca. 1940) in Nashua, New Hampshire. Drawing from

LEFT: Schaeffer House. Dining room.

BELOW: Schaeffer House. Living room.

OPPOSITE: Schaeffer House. Rear facade.

Royal Barry Wills, Walter Barker House, Nashua, New Hampshire, ca. 1940.
Entrance facade.

Barker House. Plans.

early New England two-story farmhouses with extensions that provided covered connections to the barn and stables, the form still had relevance for the harsh winters. Now the extensions became a kitchen, laundry room, and garage. At one end, the second story overhung the first floor, and large finials from the early house were attached to the corner boards, adding to the air of a house that had evolved. The massive chimney had raised pilasters, and the roof had the appropriate twelve-inch pitch of the period. As a concession to the problems of winter and snow buildup, the roof was extended on brackets and did not have gutters. Recalling the idea of a house that grew over time, the entrance of the main block was slightly off-center. The door surrounds, with pilasters and small lights over the door, borrowed from Federal-era New Hampshire houses. The plan, while drawing from the past, was very contemporary with its large hall that ran the depth of the house, and bow windows that opened the large living room and dining room onto the rear garden. A book published by the Wills firm noted that bow windows "were not found in the early houses," but then explained: "However, had the inhabitants had our efficient heating sys-

tems, a bow window. . . would have been used."[15] The large hall, with its wainscoting and wallpaper of early American scenes, was designed with the staircase tucked in the front corner, only the newel posts were turned and the balusters were appropriately simple, indicating that this was a farm house. As in other houses where Wills retained control of the design, proper reproduction hardware was employed and the dining room had a built-in corner cabinet.

Barker House. Living room.

Despite his large volume of work, Wills kept his firm small, usually employing only a few associates, such as Warren J. Rhoter and his son Richard Wills, who joined in 1952. In 1957, the company became Royal Barry Wills Associates, and a third generation, Jessica Barry Wills, came aboard in 1986. With offices in Boston and New Castle, Maine, the firm has major projects across the country, though houses continue to be its specialty.

The Herbert S. Pheeney House (1999) in Osterville on Cape Cod is clearly inspired by Federal-era houses of the Cape and Nantucket. Set back from the road with a four-hundred-foot drive, a grassy forecourt greets the visitor. The main block

has a chimney on each end and a slightly off-center entrance with a fan light. Gray shingles, rather than clapboard, were employed on the exterior in keeping with local traditions. The wings contain various family rooms and the garage is treated as a stable. A formal garden with parterres is to the rear, as is a swimming pool. The designs of the octagonal garden and pool structures can be traced to Mount Vernon. The interior contains a mixture of features that are common to the twentieth century, including a media room, and there are large windows to the rear for light and for connections to the garden. Richard Fitz Gerald advised on the interior, resulting in a mixture of colonial- and Federal-era furnishings supplemented with nineteenth-century American art. The hall contains a mural illustrating local Osterville history, painted by New York artist James Alan Smith. The floor has wide boards and hand-stenciled patterns derived, again, from the Federal period. Evoking the oriental connections of many

OPPOSITE, TOP: Barker House. Entrance hall.

OPPOSITE, BOTTOM: Barker House. Study.

BELOW: Richard Wills of Royal Barry Wills Associates, Herbert S. Pheeney House, Osterville, Massachusetts, 1999. Entrance facade.

Pheeney House. Rear facade.

Cape Cod ship captains of the Federal period, the dining room's walls are covered in a hand-painted Chinese-styled wallpaper. All of the house's front-facing windows have interior shutters that fold back into recesses in the deep wall. The house is impressive but also reticent in the best Royal Barry Wills tradition.[16]

JIMMY MEANS AND GEORGIA CONTINUATIONS

Continuity, rather than rupture, characterizes an Atlanta group of architects sometimes known as the Georgia Classicists. Their roots go back to the early twentieth century and the architectural firm Neel Reid began and which Philip Shutze took over as main designer.

James Collier Means, known in Southern fashion as "Jimmy," was born outside Atlanta in 1904, and his family moved to town when he was two years old, his father having established a contracting business there. The young Means took some mechanical drawing courses and, in 1917, began working part-time as an office boy for Reid's firm. He graduated from high school and briefly studied architecture at Georgia Tech but then decided to study on the job and, thus, became a full-time draftsman for the firm. He worked directly under the office's two main designers at the time,

LEFT, TOP: Pheeney House. Entrance hall.

LEFT, BOTTOM: Pheeney House. Dining room.

BELOW: Pheeney House. Library.

Reid and Shutze, and became a leading draftsman. He participated in the design of many of Shutze's great works and developed a reputation for his precise drafting style and his eye for detail. All traditional architectural practices had great libraries, and Means built his own personal library of books on colonial-era architecture. A trademark of Means's work was not just precise detail but an understanding of classical proportions and the use of controlling lines and geometrical order for facades and plans. In 1952, after Shutze retired, Means essentially continued the work of Shutze and his partners. In 1954, after a brief partnership with Edward Vason Jones, Means opened his own office. By the time of his death, in 1979, he had designed over a hundred houses.[17]

Means's house for Thomas E. and Peggy Sheffield Martin, built between 1964 and 1966 in the Buckhead section of Atlanta, is one of his largest commissions and illuminates his all-encompassing approach to design. The site, located in a meadow near a creek and a riding club, was one of several scouted by the Martins and Means. When Means saw the site with its great oak tree, he said, "This is what you want." The oak became the axis of the house. The Martins had attended college in Virginia: Tom at the University of Virginia, and Peggy at Sweet Briar College. They wanted a house with Virginia associations, or as she told Means, "We need a James River house." Means sent them on a trip to visit such venerable Virginia houses as the Shirley, Westover, Wilton, Carter's Grove, and the ruins at Rosewell. Additionally, Means suggested that Peggy Martin should attend the Colonial Williamsburg Antique Forum, which she did for several years. This proved important to the selection of the interiors and furnishings.[18]

Means's design went through several stages. He initially produced a design with wings and hyphens, which Peggy Martin described as "containing more room than the main house." The Martins eventually settled on Means's third design treatment. The house was large with nearly 7,000 square feet. The main block measured fifty-nine by forty-five feet. The main, or approach, facade recalls Carter's Grove's north, or five-bay, elevation, as does the brick door surrounds, though the window details come from Westover. The other facade, which acts as the entrance, is simpler. In spite of the high cost, Means insisted on a rubbed-brick belt course and window arches. The wings were Virginian, with clipped gable ends. Old bricks, acquired from a number of historical sites in Virginia such as Rosewell and the university, were placed in the walls to symbolize the house's roots. Wood beams from an old factory that Means had stockpiled were also used in construction. A walled garden was placed next to the west wing, the location of the master bedroom, and Means employed serpentine brick walls there that recalled Jefferson's garden enclosures at the University of Virginia. Edith Henderson was responsible for the garden's layout and plantings.

James Collier Means, Thomas Martin House, Atlanta, Georgia, 1964–66. Plan.

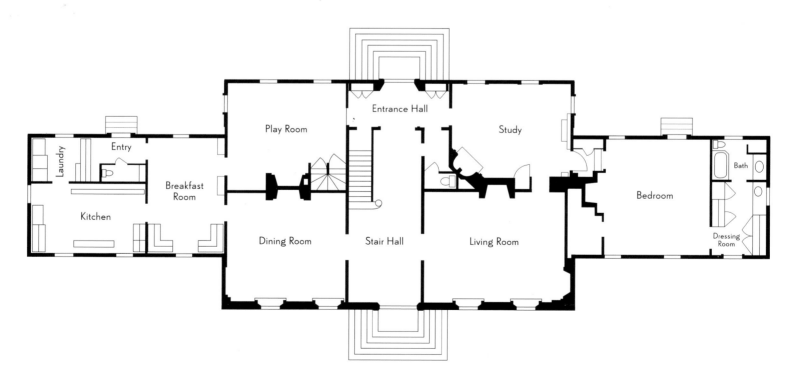

TOP: Martin House. Southwest facade.

BOTTOM: Martin House. Southeast facade.

TOP: Martin House. Dining room.

BOTTOM: Martin House. Entrance hall.

Inside the house, the room arrangement resembles a number of Virginia's double-pile house plans, though with a few key changes. Means's entrance hall, or vestibule, is more clearly separated from the stair hall. The Martins tried to save some money by reducing the ceiling height to eleven feet. Means's response to their cost-cutting attempts was, "I want your children to know I am not building a barn." However, the Martins prevailed in several places, including the hall, which Means designed with paneling recalling Carter's Grove. Peggy Martin, working with David Richmond Byers, a noted Atlanta decorator (who met with Means's approval), simplified the hall. Byers had studied at the University of Virginia and did several rooms at the White House during Jimmy Carter's presidency. Means had suggested Wilton as the source for the dining room, but Byers designed a new

Chinese-styled wallpaper. Most of the furnishings were either antiques collected by Peggy Martin, or reproduction designs that she and Byers selected. But, as Martin remembered, "Byers and Means did what they wanted to do." Exactly who was responsible for the wonderful paneling in the study or the other rooms remains unclear. Obviously, a calculating eye was at work. The Martins lost the battle over a few important aspects of the design. As Peggy Martin fondly recalled, "Means didn't believe in big bathrooms and closets; he was eighteenth century."[19]

OVERLEAF: Martin House. Northeast facade.

Martin House. Garden.

LOUISIANA COLONIAL:
THE CREOLE REVIVAL OF A. HAYS TOWN

The houses of the colonial French and Spanish settlers in Louisiana, Alabama, and Mississippi were forgotten for many years. In the late nineteenth century a few Southern architects began to incorporate selected colonial-era features into their designs. Then, in the 1920s and 1930s, a small revival began, primarily led by New Orleans architect Richard Koch and, later, Samuel Wilson. Key features were broad-covering roofs with deep overhangs, raised wide galleries, or balconies, and extensive use of louvers and latticework. The style went under a variety of names, including Louisiana Colonial (sometimes called "New Orleans Colonial"), the Raised Cottage, and Creole Revival. One of the masters of this Deep South idiom was A. Hays Town, who designed several hundred houses between the 1950s and the 1990s.

The career of Albert Hays Town illuminates some of the conflicting values in twentieth-century American architecture, namely the fact that in the 1930s, Town designed some of Mississippi's most striking International Style buildings.[20] Town was born in 1903 and grew up in several small towns in rural Louisiana. Initially, he studied engineering at a local school, but in 1921 he entered Tulane University's architecture program in New Orleans. As with all American architecture schools at that time, Tulane's program was Beaux Arts oriented.

LEFT: Martin House. Garden and northwest facade.

OVERLEAF: A. Hays Town, Dr. Charles Greeson House, Baton Rouge, Louisiana.

However, in addition to teaching the grand classical system, some of the instructors were involved in preservation and documenting the local vernacular. While in school, Town worked for Richard Koch. Upon graduation, in 1926, Town accepted a position with the Jackson, Mississippi, architect N. W. Overstreet. In the early 1930s, he became a partner in Overstreet's office. The Great Depression forced him to search for supplementary employment, and in 1933 Town was selected to head the HABS survey team in Mississippi. The documentary research and measured drawings that Town and his team carried out in Mississippi became a model nationwide and allowed Town to explore local historical models. However, the application of this learning was put on hold as Overstreet and Town soon became involved in a large project for a group of school buildings that would be constructed across the state with federal funds during the latter part of the 1930s. Striking in their bold modernist imagery and employment of concrete, Town's schools were prominently pictured in leading architectural journals, and even Lewis Mumford, writing in *The New Yorker,* sang their praises.[21]

For family reasons, Town relocated in 1939 to Baton Rouge, Louisiana, and opened an architectural office. His work in the years that followed includes extensive commercial and public buildings and some houses. By the late 1960s, Town had grown dissatisfied with the direction of American modernism, and was ready to move beyond commonplace commercial structures. Always interested in the historical and local vernacular elements of house design, Town shifted the focus of his practice to residential work and, in the ensuing twenty years, developed a reputation as the "Master of Creole Architecture," or the "Master of Louisiana Style."[22]

The house that Town designed in 1978 for Dr. and Mrs. Charles Greeson in Baton Rouge exemplifies his appreciation of the French colonial. Town called himself "a good psychologist," and he tried to match houses to clients' personalities, and he listened intently to his clients. Seeing the sketches for the house, Greeson said, "It was as though he had read your mind."[23] Town showed the Greesons several of his earlier houses and then created for them a version of the raised Creole cottage. The basic model for the design was the Pitot House in New Orleans, one of the few late-eighteenth-century houses to survive. With its raised balcony supported on heavy piers and thin upper columns and stucco exterior, the Pitot House's origins lie in the West Indies. Town essentially adopted the Pitot's facade for the Greeson House but made it more elegant, using

Roman Doric lower columns to support the thinner piers above. Tall window-doors with shutters recall the original environmental reason for the house's form (ample ventilation of the interior), though at present air conditioning is mandatory. Other portions of the exterior are clad in brick, and the walled courtyard with the birdbath fountain recalls the courtyards of the French Quarter of New Orleans. Town also provided the landscape plan that included a small allée of crepe myrtles.

A signature element of Town's style was the use of old materials—bricks, timbers, tiles, and details salvaged from demolished buildings. If these were not available, Town taught his workmen "antiquing" techniques. The interior of the Greeson House features heavy beamed ceilings, paneled doors, and brick walls—some painted, others left natural. The living room hearth was always a focal point, sometimes set off with columns supporting the mantel. Town also typically played a role in the selection of furnishings for his houses, frequently supplying items he had purchased in antique shops in New Orleans or abroad. Persian carpets were preferred along with a few pieces of stylish antique

OPPOSITE: Greeson House. Garden.

RIGHT: Greeson House. Garden.

Greeson House. Entrance hall.

TOP: Greeson House. Living room.

BOTTOM: Greeson House. Entrance and porch.

TOP: Greeson House. Side hall.

BOTTOM: Greeson House. Porch.

furniture. He liked religious icons from Mexico and Spain, as well as porcelain, various kinds of jugs, and landscape paintings. As with the design of the house itself, the furniture and art was a mixture of ideas belonging to designer and client, but, as mentioned, Town always had sympathy for the client's taste. Speaking of their affinity for the house and their recollection of Town, Dr. Charles Greeson remarked, "No matter how much we love our house, it will always be one of Mr. Town's children."24

POSTMODERN COLONIAL: HUGH NEWELL JACOBSEN

The Stewart Greene House by Hugh Newell Jacobsen reveals a new appreciation of historical forms that characterized certain aspects of postmodernism as it developed in the 1970s and afterwards. Jacobsen emerged on the architectural scene as a committed modernist but, over time, he progressively embraced certain aspects of Early American architecture; the result is what might be considered a postmodern Colonial Revival idiom.

Hugh Newell Jacobsen, Greene House, Eastern Shore, Maryland, 1992. View
of north facade from Chesapeake Bay.

Greene House. North facade.

Greene House. South facade.

Born in Grand Rapids, Michigan, Jacobsen has suffered from dyslexia all of his life. Unable to master the traditional architectural requirements of math and physics, he majored in painting and worked for a period as a portrait painter. He was finally accepted into Yale University's architecture program and came under the influence of architect and educator Louis Kahn (1901–74), whose investigation of archaic forms left an impression. After graduation, in 1955, Jacobsen worked for Philip Johnson, who, in retreat from hard-edged modernism, had begun to introduce a new decorative twist to his work. In 1958 Jacobsen opened an office in Washington, D.C. In the 1960s, under the influence of projects by Robert Venturi and Edward Larrabee Barnes, which emphasized peaked or gabled roofs (instead of the mandatory flat roof), Jacobsen began to experiment. He also became involved in preservation, carrying out a restoration of the Renwick Art Gallery in Washington, D.C., and later making additions to the United States Capitol. Although responsible for large projects, Jacobsen earned his reputation from his designs for a number of elegant houses. By the mid-1970s, Jacobsen arrived at his sig-

nature house form, a series of pavilions with gabled roofs. Also at this time, historical imagery began to be an element in his work.

"I abstract a lot of my work from the vernacular, and then I clean it up," Jacobsen has said. He is also well known for his emphasis on order, or as he explains it: "You see, I am symmetrical. You are symmetrical. Some people call me a formal architect, because I make symmetrical houses—but really, the houses are like you and me." This emphasis on symmetry, and the architectural imagery of some of Jacobsen's houses, has led to his work being called Palladian. One critic claimed Jacobsen's architecture was not just decoration, but "a genuine attempt to revive classical architectural concepts." The critic cited symmetry, proportion, and employment of squares, cubes, and mathematical ratios as elements of Jacobsen's work.[25] Historicism also enters Jacobsen's work, often in the form of overt references to James River Georgian, Pennsylvania German Colonial, Spanish Mission, Greek Revival, and Cape Cod cottages. But Jacobsen also designed convincing purely modernist houses. Even in his overtly historical designs, a modern sensibility emerges with the sparseness of furnishings, large window openings, and minimal trim.

Greene House. South facade.

The Greene House on Maryland's Eastern Shore of the Chesapeake Bay sits in an area settled in the seventeenth and eighteenth centuries. Several building types were common to the area, including the extended house composed of a series of rooms. The early settlers also built dispersed single-room structures for dwelling, farming, and storage. For the Greene House, Jacobsen essentially abstracted these building forms and created a new composition. Rigidly symmetrical, the front entry pavilion is separated from the five-part main house, and pushed forward to act as a welcoming element. Anchoring the composition is the large fireplace and hearth of the central pavilion, which is approached through a paneled entry hall. The cross axis exposes the house to the visitor at the approach to the three-story-tall space of the main room. Large corner windows open the space to the terrace and river beyond. The other pavilions are used as music and lounge spaces and contain the dining room, kitchen, bedrooms,

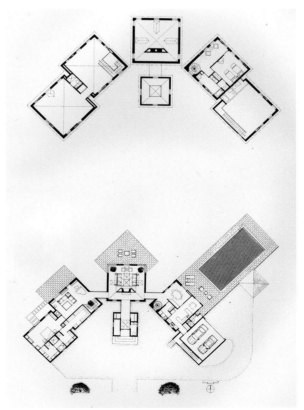

Greene House. Plans.

ABOVE: Greene House.

OPPOSITE: Greene House. Living room.

and garage. Interior furnishings are very modern, but there is a classic sense of balance.[26]

The simple boxlike forms of the Greene House, clad in white clapboard, impart a timeless and vernacular feel to the design. The employment of square nine-paned windows (with one exception), and their placement (both symmetrically and asymmetrically), provides unity and variety. Jacobsen's work exudes a somewhat sly whimsy, not as a joke but as a modern reinterpretation of a timeless building.

MASTER OF THE CLASSICAL COLONIAL: ALLAN GREENBERG

For Allan Greenberg, the various colonial-period styles and their revivals are part of a very old process with links to antiquity that carry multiple and very profound meanings still valid in the present: "Classical architecture has remained viable—and classical buildings endure for centuries—because it is not a style; it is a comprehensive language of architectural form with a grammar and vocabulary to articulate form and meaning. . . . For the founders of the United States,

OPPOSITE: Greene House. Staircase in east wing.

ABOVE: Greene House. Staircase in west wing.

BELOW: Greene House. Living room.

Allan Greenberg, Farmhouse, Greenwich, Connecticut, 1979–83.
Entrance facade.

classical architecture offered the only architectural language that could express the new republic's democratic ideal."[27] In addition to running a major architectural practice with offices in Washington, D.C., New York, and Greenwich, Connecticut, Greenberg wrote on the British classicist Edwin Lutyens, and also the architecture of George Washington. Mount Vernon is a touchstone for Greenberg, and he views it not as just architecture but as architecture that is expressive of political ideals. Greenberg sees in the house a balance between symmetry and asymmetry that reveals Washington's humanistic qualities. This interaction of opposites in the house and also in Mount Vernon's farms, gardens, and landscape was for Greenberg "a prospect of human aspiration in harmonious alignment with nature."[28]

Greenberg was born in 1938 in Johannesburg, South Africa, and studied architecture at the University of Witwatersrand, a school that followed classical models. He then worked for the Danish modernist Jorn Utzon, before coming to the United States to attend graduate architecture school at Yale University. Le Corbusier was one of his heroes, and Greenberg still expresses admiration for his buildings and for those of contemporary modernists such as Norman Foster. But as he went on to work in Connecticut's New Haven Redevelopment Agency, and then teach at Yale and other schools, Greenberg became convinced that classicism offered a viable alternative to the modernist morass. Some of his early work in the 1970s, such as the addition to the State Library and Supreme Court Building in Hartford, contained postmodernist elements, but as his confidence grew, he more fully engaged the classical past. Greenberg has designed rooms for the Department of State in Washington, D.C., a number of residences, and commercial buildings for Bergdorf Goodman and others.

Greenberg's best-known work, and indeed a defining building for American architecture in the last half-century, is the Farmhouse (1979–83) at White Birch Farm in Greenwich, Connecticut. Neither a modern house nor an ironical postmodern parody, it was the first openly historicist design by an architect who, though young, could be considered a member of the elite East Coast architectural establishment. The owners were avid collectors of Art Deco and Pop art. In the early 1970s, they built a Robert Venturi–John Rauch house that contained references to Art Deco, suburban doctor's offices, and tract housing; it was Pop architecture. By the late 1970s, the owners had begun to assemble a collection of Early Amer-

ican art and antiques and asked Venturi to design an addition to the house. Dissatisfied with the solution he proposed, they decided to construct a new and larger house on the property. Influenced by the revival of interest in late-nineteenth-century academic and Colonial Revival architecture, and being familiar with houses like Hill-Stead in nearby Farmington, Connecticut, they wanted an architect who could design a house "to look like Mount Vernon and also to resemble some of the airy Classical houses of McKim, Mead & White." The owners contacted the architect Philip Johnson and the Museum of Modern Art's curator, Arthur Drexler; they both suggested Greenberg. After Greenberg had produced his design, Venturi and his partners produced a whimsical play emphasizing the asymmetry of the Potomac River landmark. Deborah Nevins, the late Russell Page, and Jed Johnson assisted Greenberg on the project. A major group of skilled wood turners and carvers provided many of the details.[29]

Greenberg's Mount Vernon in Greenwich is not a copy of the original, but a corrected version—ultimately more classical than Washington ever created. This is important since, as Greenberg later wrote, the asymmetrical distribution of openings and other elements at Mount Vernon, such as the fenestration on all the facades, provides insight into Washington's vision and decision not to create a perfect design. Washington was hampered by a preexisting building that he made major additions to and he resolutely never destroyed the old for the new. Greenberg started with a blank slate and consequently created a fully symmetrical structure that bows to the original in its details, such as the rusticated wood siding. Greenberg alludes to Mount Vernon's asymmetry by aligning the window edges of the entrance facade, creating a syncopated rhythm between the first and second floor. The

RIGHT: Farmhouse. Garden portico.

OVERLEAF: Farmhouse. Garden facade.

house is a five-part composition as is Mount Vernon; the main block is connected by arcades to the dependencies but in Connecticut one contains a pool, the other garages. In addition to the symmetry, Greenberg's Mount Vernon has a colonnade of twelve Roman Doric columns placed in pairs, instead of Washington's rather spindly eight Tuscan piers. The floating, or unanchored, pediment on the land/entrance facade at Mount Vernon is corrected in Connecticut: the pediment is properly supported by large console scrolls. Greenberg excels at details, creating more correct portions for the arcade, and both the entrance and garden elevation doors have very robust pediments and surrounds—not the simplicity and modesty of Washington's.

BELOW: Farmhouse. Family room.

RIGHT: Farmhouse. Entrance hall.

Washington's Mount Vernon, in spite of what photographs might indicate, is a small house, cramped in many areas, while Greenberg's Greenwich house is large and ample, and is a fully modern structure. The hall, with a staircase modeled on the Virginia example, is at the center, but it is larger and more open and light filled with a great staircase window. The owner's taste is evident in the choices of art that adorn the walls of the living room, a collection that includes various works by Andy Warhol and Early American paintings. But they are offset with interior paneling, trim, moldings, and wall treatments such as the Chinese wallpaper in the dining room. One element that marks a Greenberg design is his moldings, which have been compared to those utilized by Jefferson.[30] The consequence is a robustness of detail, a richness that surrounds many of the doors, fireplaces, and ceilings.

ROBERT A. M. STERN AND THE USABLE PAST

Of the present-day architects designing in Colonial Revival and other historicist idioms, Robert A. M. Stern is the superstar. Born in New York in 1938, he trained first at Columbia and then at Yale, where he came under the influence of Vincent Scully and Philip Johnson. Stern has been a ubiquitous presence on the American architectural scene since the 1960s. The head of a large architectural practice with hundreds of projects and buildings to his credit, he is also a scholar and critic with numerous books published, including a series on the architecture of New York City. He has also found time to teach at Columbia University and is currently Dean of Architecture at Yale University. His most public presentation was a PBS television series and book, *Pride of Place* (1986), which spelled out his position on American architecture. In it, Stern recounts growing up in Manhattan and loving the older buildings, telling of how he could not "understand . . . why the new buildings of the fifties were so drained of quality and of aspiration, why they were so bland, so inarticulate, and so boring." Yet Stern is not entirely negative on all modern architects—for instance, Frank Lloyd Wright and Louis Kahn receive his praise—but he argues that respect should be granted to the much longer American tradition that looked to history for inspiration. Heretically, Stern closes *Pride of Place* with a paradigm for American life: "However idealized, Williamsburg's past is an eminently usable one"; it is not simply a history lesson, he adds, but "a textbook for the future."[31]

Stern initially began as a postmodernist and created a variety of high-profile houses with cartoonish and Venturi-esque features that drew tentatively upon the past. By the late 1970s, he began to recover from the quest to be, as he noted, " 'original,' 'interesting,' and most especially 'modern,' " and, as he relates further, "discovered the vitality of forms rooted in tradition." Stern has called his approach "new-old" and "Modern Traditionalism."[32] He and his firm have designed in a tremendous range of historical idioms, from the stripped classicism of the 1930s, popularized by Paul Cret, to English half-timber, to Jeffersonian classicism, to many varieties of Shingle Style, or, as it was known in the 1880s, "modernized colonial."

The Frederick Baron–Lisa Blue residence (2002) at Preston Hollow in Dallas, Texas, illustrates Stern's approach and the continuing relationship of Colonial Revival to English sources. Located on a lot of nine acres, the site was chosen by Stern, and his firm did the landscaping. The house was sited "so that it would take command of the site in the way that classical buildings can do." Arranged around a series of outdoor courtyards, an axial sequence leads from the square

Robert A. M. Stern, Baron-Blue House, Dallas, Texas, 2002. View into dining room.

Baron-Blue House. Entrance facade.

motor court, through the centrally located living room, to a lawn and creek, while formal terraces and gardens open off the other two sides. The axis of the enfilade that continues through the house and the nearly identical wings is not particularly English, but American-derived through French architectural training. English architects might aspire to such order but the realities of the layout are closed spaces and a complicated circulation path. The process of order that Stern imposed reveals the lingering impact of Beaux Arts planning on American architectural education.[33] Stern describes the design as "English Regency sifted through American Federal." With its red brick and light-colored trim—classical details— and wings, the house would fit into the James River Georgian mode, though at 21,000 square feet the Dallas house far surpasses any American house of the eighteenth and early nineteenth centuries, and is characteristic of its English country-house scale. Many of the exterior details can be traced to English pattern books. Stern explained: "We looked to the somewhat attenuated vocabularies of Sir John Soane,

Bulfinch, Latrobe, Robert Mills, William Strickland, and other early-nineteenth-century architects." He also notes John Russell Pope, adding that they "studied precedents exhaustively and tried to make the traditions our own." The exterior order is based upon the Temple of Winds in Athens but, as Stern notes, it is more stylized, as by Robert Mills or Soane."

The entry hall with its curved, suspended staircase and classical detailing looks back to American Federal and English models of the same period. The low vault recalls Soane and early-twentieth-century revival architects. Stern credits the marble floor to Lutyens, but Ogden Codman Jr. actually reintroduced the pattern. "Millsonian," or abstracted Temple of the Winds, pilasters articulate the living room. The library contains Corinthian pilasters, which have been stylized with Texas wildflowers. The conservatory's treillage was a favorite motif of Codman and his disciple Elsie de Wolfe. As Stern openly acknowledges, the Baron-Blue House derives

Baron-Blue House. Garden facade.

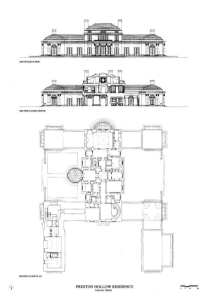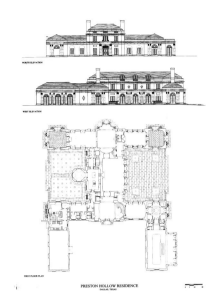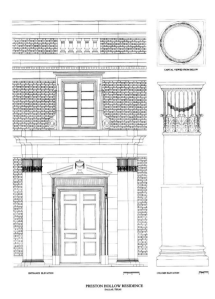

Baron-Blue House. Plans and details.

from a close study of history, but it is a new interpretation of that past.

NEW OLD FOGIES: FAIRFAX AND SAMMONS

Overlooking Lake Otsego in Cooperstown, New York, Farmlands reads as a permanent part of its site, almost as if it had been built sometime between 1800 and 1820. One might even suspect that it is the work of Benjamin Henry Latrobe or one of his apprentices, or that the owner and/or builder had been south to Philadelphia or Baltimore and observed the new trends in young American architecture. But close inspection reveals unusually crisp detailing, as if the house might have been renewed. The truth, however, is that Farmlands was completed in 2002. Anne Fairfax and Richard Sammons, the architects of Farmlands, intended to be respectful of local traditions. A frame house that stood on the site was removed but some elements, such as the entry door and surrounds, were employed in the new structure. In volume and size, the new house is larger but recalls the older version.

Cooperstown, founded in 1787, is located in the Mohawk Valley near the middle of New York State and occupies an important place in American lore as not only the location of

the Baseball Hall of Fame but the home of James Fenimore Cooper, who created one of the country's great fictional myths — the frontiersman Natty Bumppo of *Last of the Mohicans* (1826) — and authored the other novels in the "Leatherstocking" saga. Cooper lived substantial portions of his life in Cooperstown and in his writings portrayed its natural features such as Lake Otsego, which he named Glimmerglass Lake. Many of Cooperstown's original residents came from Connecticut and New York, and houses constructed of local rubble stone with classical detailing survive, such as Woodside Hall, which inspired the architects Fairfax and Sammons. Several twentieth-century Colonial Revival buildings, such as the Farmer's Museum, revived the use of coursed stone.[34]

Richard Sammons and Anne Fairfax design traditional houses. Part of a group sometimes called "young old fogies," they are relatively youthful (in the sense that architecture is sometimes described as "an old man's game,") and, instead of following the modernist hegemony, they look to the past and colonial period architecture in particular for inspiration. Fairfax and Sammons met in architecture school at the University of Virginia in the mid-1980s and imbibed some of the postmodern currents then underway. After school, Sammons worked for the New York decorator-architect David Anthony Easton, and Fairfax worked in Hawaii on several restorations. They married and opened their practice in New York City in 1992. Both have been involved with the various classicist groups and the Prince of Wales Institute for classical architecture.[35]

Farmlands illuminates the sophistication of a younger generation of architects with Colonial precedent. Built with traditional load-bearing walls of a local blue stone that was

quarried near the site, the pieces are between ten and twelve inches thick. The stone was pried from ledges and laid in coursed rubble and leveled at every quoin. The quoins in the corners graduate and diminish in size from bottom to top. The central block of stone stands forth boldly. Shingled wings are set back on each side and the white-cedar shingles have ten-inch exposures and rose nails at their butts. The roof is New York slate. The giant portico capitals were derived from the Temple of the Winds in Athens. The unorthodox second-story porch, hung on tension rods, provides the main bedroom with a great outdoor view, but also is a subtle homage to the porches on Jefferson's pavilions at the University of Virginia. The recessed, arched Palladian windows on the house's lakeside were also a motif favored by Federal-era designers such as Latrobe and Bulfinch. In this case, Sammons looked closely at Woodlands, a great Federal-era house in Philadelphia, though such treatments can be traced back to Robert Adam, Lord Burlington, and Palladio.[36]

Many large American manor houses of the early-nineteenth century had two facades, as does Farmlands; however, instead of entering through the giant portico on the south facade, which overlooks the lake, as one might have done, the other, or north, facade acts as the major entrance. Slightly more subdued, the north or entrance facade is a five-part composition consisting of a central pavilion, hyphens, and two more pavilions of stone, and then clapboarded wings. This contrast between the two facades indicates that Farmlands was conceived as a whole and was not the product of additions, as might be common to a house of 1820.

Inside the house, the same historical sophistication continues. The entry hall recalls Federal examples with its screened niche and suspended staircase, and also the work of William Lawrence Bottomley from the 1920s and 1930s. Sammons conceived of the space "as a natural history museum a la Monticello." Across the lake side of the house, the rooms are arranged enfilade. Sally Dinkle Giordano assisted on the interior decoration. The drawing room is paneled and contains carefully detailed windows with Ionic columns. Balancing the drawing room, and with an equal vista to the lake, is the dining room that has reproduction French Zuber block-printed wallpaper appropriate to the retrospective vision the house maintains. Located in a wing is the kitchen/family sitting

room, which contains a paneled end wall that recalls Connecticut colonial examples, in addition to a large hearth with cooking-size fireplace with crane, and Windsor chairs. Commenting on the space, Sammons noted, "No spinning wheel, but otherwise pure Wallace Nutting."[37]

Farmlands is unabashedly Colonial Revival 2002, but Fairfax and Sammons also argue, as do many of the other "young old fogies," or "reticent revolutionaries," which is another label applied to them, that their work is contemporary and offers solutions to architectural issues. Their work follows rules and looks to tradition but also expands on the past.

PAST, PRESENT, AND FUTURE

Colonial Revival remains the United States's most characteristic and popular expression, especially in the single-family house. The revival of forms, details, and styles based on Early American houses has a long history. From Sunnyside and Bremo Recess in the 1830s, to Farmlands and the Baron-Blue House in 2002, from Gloucester, Massachusetts, and Atlanta, Georgia, to San Marino, California, Colonial Revival spans the United States chronologically and geographically. Some of the houses shown reveal painstaking fidelity to the past, while others more loosely draw upon Colonial precedent. A direct line runs between the academic historicism of the H. A. C. Taylor House and Farmlands; also connected are McKim, Mead & White's modernized Colonial Revival at the Bell House and Hugh Newell Jacobsen's abstracted Colonial

OPPOSITE: Anne Fairfax and Richard Sammons, Farmlands, Cooperstown, New York, 2002. Garden facade.

RIGHT: Farmlands. Library.

OVERLEAF, LEFT: Farmlands. Entrance hall.

OVERLEAF, RIGHT: Farmlands. Sitting room.

Farmlands. Detail of dining room.

Revival at the Greene House. Pattern appropriation, fidelity to detail, and artistic reinterpretation, all found in the 1830s, remain approaches today

Colonial Revival, in spite of being declared dead for the past half-century and more, continues today. Certainly there are other expressions in American houses; in recent years craftsman, ranch, and even modern tract houses have become objects of desire. But the long-standing popularity of recalling the American past has never disappeared. "Imitation is the sincerest form of flattery" is an aphorism that assists in understanding the historicism underlying the revival of Early American historical elements. The reasons are manifold and embody many popular images that include home, hearth, safety, and patriotism.[38]

Colonial Revival revels in imitation and it is aligned with a national stereotype that has been characterized as "the plas-

OPPOSITE: Farmlands. Dining room.

RIGHT: Farmlands. Detail of second-floor porch.

ter cast syndrome" and "reassurance through imitation." The critique of the American penchant for theme parks, limited-edition genuine copies, and the fake-over-the-real can be devastating and amusing. Certainly the commercialization of the past, the tacky pastiches, and the repulsive patriotic sentimentalizing can drive one quite quickly into the modernist camp. However, imitating, copying, or drawing upon the past and precedent has a very long history in art and architecture, and even the most ardent American modernists— whether of the 1900s or the 1950s—owed substantial debts to what had come before. One must ask, what is the problem? Taste is certainly part of the issue, but the fact remains that everything created owes some debt to the past. There is good Colonial Revival and bad, just as there is good and bad modern.[39]

The past is malleable and changeable; new ideas and concepts, along with rediscovered forms, details, and objects, appear, reappear, and disappear. The past, and what we think we know of it, is a construction that changes over time. History concerns itself with past events and objects (such as buildings), and it attempts to interpret them for the present day. From Colonial Revival, lessons might be learned about America's image of the house and what Americans find comfortable and appealing in relation to it. While Colonial Revival is not the only American architecture, it has proved to be a potent source of design for the American house, one that will continue with more acts to come.

Notes

INTRODUCTION

1. Wallace Nutting, *Massachusetts Beautiful* (Garden City: Old America Co., 1923), 125.
2. Hugh Morrison, *Early American Architecture* (New York: Oxford University Press, 1952), 3–4.
3. Thomas Jefferson to Dr. James Mease, September 26, 1825, *The Writings of Thomas Jefferson*, vol. 16, ed. Andrew A. Lipscomb (Washington, D.C.: Thomas Jefferson Memorial Association, 1905), 123.
4. As examples see: Rodris Roth, "The New England, or 'Old Tyme,' Kitchen Exhibit at Nineteenth-Century Fairs," and Beverly Seaton, "A Pedigree for a New Century: The Colonial Experience in Popular Historical Novels, 1890–1910," in *The Colonial Revival in America*, ed. Alan Axelrod (New York: W. W. Norton, 1985), 159–83, 278–93.
5. Edwin Howland Blashfield, *Mural Painting in America* (New York: Scribner's, 1913), 8.
6. Alfred Busselle, "Domestic Quality in School Design," *Architecture* 43 (April 1921): 121; and "Our School Architecture," *Architecture* 42 (November 1920): 325.
7. Harry B. Henderson III, *Versions of the Past: The Historical Imagination in American Fiction* (New York: Oxford University Press, 1974); and George Dekker, *The American Historical Romance* (New York: Cambridge University Press, 1987).
8. Kenneth Ames, introduction to *The Colonial Revival in America*, ed. Axelrod, 10–13.
9. T. J. Jackson Lears, *No Place of Grace: Antimodernism and the Transformation of American Culture 1880–1920* (New York: Random House, 1981).
10. Michael Kammen, *Mystic Chords of Memory: The Transformation in American Culture* (New York: Knopf, 1991), 626.
11. David Lowenthal, *The Past Is a Foreign Country* (Cambridge: Cambridge University Press, 1985), 196–97.
12. Frank Lloyd Wright, "Architect, Architecture, and the Client" (1896), in *Frank Lloyd Wright Collected Writings*, vol. 1, ed. Bruce Brooks Pfeiffer (New York: Rizzoli, 1992), 30.
13. Lewis Mumford, *Sticks and Stones* (New York: Boni and Liveright, 1924), 50.
14. Charles Taylor, *The Ethics of Authenticity* (Cambridge, Mass.: Harvard University Press, 1991).

CHAPTER I

1. Thomas Jefferson, *Notes on the State of Virginia*, ed. William Peden (1781, 1787; reprint, Chapel Hill: University of North Carolina Press, 1954), 152–53, 154; and Mrs. L. (Louisa) C. Tuthill, *History of architecture from the earliest times: its present condition in Europe and the United States* (1848; reprint, New York: Garland, 1988), 243, 258. See, Sarah Allaback, "Louisa Tuthill, Ithiel Town, and the Beginnings of Architectural History Writing in America," in Kenneth Hafertepe and James F. O'Gorman, *American Architects and Their Books to 1848* (Amherst: University of Massachusetts Press, 2001), 199–215.
2. Of the few studies in this area see: Donald Wesley Matheson, "'To Grandfather's House We'll Go': New England and the Colonial Revival of the Mid-Nineteenth Century" (master's thesis, University of Virginia, 1991); W. Barksdale Maynard, "'Best, Lowliest Style!' The Early-Nineteenth-Century Rediscovery of American Colonial Architecture," *Journal of the Society of Architectural Historians* 59, no. 3 (September 2000): 338–57; Maynard, *Architecture in the United States 1800–1850* (New Haven: Yale University Press, 2002); and William B. Rhoads, *The Colonial Revival*, 2 vols. (New York: Garland, 1977), chap. 1–2.
3. David James Kiracofe, "The Jamestown Jubilees," *Virginia Magazine of History and Biography* 110 no. 1 (2002): 35–68. See also Michael Kammen, *A Season of Youth: The American Revolution and the Historical Imagination* (1978; reprint, Ithaca, N.Y.: Cornell University Press, 1988); and Eric Hobsbawn and Terence Ranger, eds., *Invention of Tradition* (New York: Cambridge University Press, 1992).
4. *The Compact Edition of the Oxford English Dictionary* (Oxford: Oxford University Press, 1971), 3114.
5. Augustus Welby Northmore Pugin, *The True Principles of Pointed or Christian Architecture* (London: J. Weale, 1841), 56–57.
6. John Ruskin, *The Seven Lamps of Architecture* (New York: J. Wiley, 1849), 183. Roger Stein, *John Ruskin and Aesthetic Thought in America, 1840–1900* (Cambridge, Mass.: Harvard University Press, 1967).
7. Owen Jones, *The Grammar of Ornament* (London: Day and Son, 1856), 5.
8. Eugene-Emmanuel Viollet-le-Duc, *Discourses on Architecture*, trans. Benjamin Bucknall (1889; reprint, New York: Grove Press, 1959), 244.
9. Vivien Green Fryd, *Art and Empire: The Politics of Ethnicity in the United States Capitol, 1815–1860* (New Haven: Yale University Press, 1992).
10. Agnes Addison Gilchrist, *William Strickland, Architect and Engineer, 1788–1854* (New York: Da Capo, 1969), 78–79; Charlene Mires, *Independence Hall in American Memory* (Philadelphia: University of Pennsylvania Press, 2002), 73–77; and John Maass, "Architecture and Americanism or Pastiches of Independence Hall," *Historic Preservation* 22, no. 2 (April–June 1970): 17–25.
11. Nathaniel Hawthorne, *The Marble Faun* (1860; reprint, Oxford: Oxford University Press, 2002), 4.
12. Henry Wadsworth Longfellow, *Kavanagh* (1849; reprint, New Haven: College and University Press, 1965), 85–86.
13. Henry Wadsworth Longfellow, "To A Child," in *The Poetical Works of Henry Wadsworth Longfellow* (Boston: Houghton Mifflin, 1881), 129. For information on the house I am indebted to Sarah H. Heald, "'To Keep up the Delusion': Henry W. Longfellow's House and Furnishings," forthcoming.
14. Longfellow to George Washington Greene, May 28, 1877, *Letters of Henry Wadsworth Longfellow*, vol. 6, ed. A. Hilen (Cambridge, Mass.: Harvard University Press, 1982), 273–74.
15. Henry Wadsworth Longfellow, *The Poetical Works of Henry Wadsworth Longfellow* (Boston: Houghton Mifflin, 1881), 304. See also Christopher Monkhouse, "The Spinning Wheel as Artifact, Symbol, and Source of Design," in *Victorian Furniture: Essays from a Victorian Society Autumn Symposium*, ed. Kenneth L. Ames (Philadelphia: Victorian Society in America, 1982), 153–72.
16. *Gleason's Pictorial Drawing Room Companion* (June 12, 1852), 376. See also Ann Leighton, *American Gardens of the Nineteenth Century* (Amherst: University of Massachusetts Press, 1987), 224–25; and Marie L. Carden and Thomas Denenberg, *Longfellow National Historical Site, Cambridge, Massachusetts, Historical Overview and Evaluation of Significance* (National Park Service, 1996), 136.
17. Quoted in Katherine Cole Stevenson and H. Ward Jandl, *Houses by Mail: A Guide to Houses from Sears, Roebuck and Company* (Washington, D.C.: Preservation Press, 1986), 285.
18. Washington Irving, "The Author's Apology" (1848), in *A History of New York*, ed. Edwin T. Bowden (New Haven: College and University Press, 1964), 351.
19. Washington Irving to Peter Irving, October 8, 1835, in *Washington Irving Letters*, vol. 2, Ralph M. Alderman et al. (Boston: Twayne Publishers, 1979), 834; and Irving to George Harvey, November 23, 1835, 844–45. Letter of Geoffrey Crayon to the editor of the *Knickerbocker Magazine* (March 1839), *Washington Irving Miscellaneous Writings, 1803–1859*, vol. 2 (Boston: Twayne Publishers, 1981), 103.

20. "Sunnyside, the Home of Washington Irving," *Harper's* 14 (December 1856): 7, 10; "Authors," *Harper's* 16 (April 1858): 792. Andrew Jackson Downing, *Treatise on the Theory and Practice of Landscape Gardening Adapted to North America* (New York: Wiley & Putnam, 1841). See also Stephen Bann, "The Historical Composition of Place: Byron and Scott," in *Clothing of Clio* (Cambridge: Cambridge University Press, 1984).

21. John Hartwell Cocke to Charles Tyler Botts, 1844, Cocke Papers, Special Collections, University of Virginia Library. See Tatiana S. Durlin, "Bremo Recess: A Colonial Jacobean Revival" (master's thesis, University of Virginia, 1990); and Charles E. Brownell, "Bremo Recess," in Brownell, Calder Loth, William Rasmussen, and Richard Guy Wilson, *The Making of Virginia Architecture* (Richmond: Virginia Museum of Fine Arts, 1992), 258–59.

22. [Arthur Gilman], "Architecture in the United States," *North American Review* 58 (April 1844): 436–80. Roger G. Reed, "Paris in the New World: Arthur Gilman's Vision of American Architecture," *Nineteenth Century* 23, no. 1 (Spring 2003): 18–29.

23. Barbara J. Mitnick, ed., *George Washington: American Symbol* (New York: Hudson Hills Press, 1999); and Karal Ann Marling, *George Washington Slept Here: Colonial Revivals and American Culture, 1876–1986* (Cambridge, Mass.: Harvard University Press, 1988).

24. Charles B. Hosmer Jr., *Presence of the Past: A History of the Historic Preservation Movement in the United States before Williamsburg* (New York: Putman, 1965), 35–36.

25. Hosmer, *Presence of the Past,* 42. See also Jean B. Lee, "Historical Memory, Sectional Strife, and the American Mecca, Mount Vernon, 1783–1853," *Virginia Magazine of History and Biography* 109, no. 3 (2001): 255–300. On Mount Vernon see: Allan Greenberg, *George Washington Architect* (New York and London: Andreas Papadakis Publisher, 1999); Wendell Garrett, ed., *George Washington's Mount Vernon,* (New York: Monacelli Press, 1998); and Robert F. Dalzell Jr. and Lee Baldwin Dalzell, *George Washington's Mount Vernon: At Home in Revolutionary America* (New York: Oxford University Press, 1998).

26. Edward Everett, *Oration on the Character of Washington* (Boston: Little, Brown, 1913), 23, 24, 25. See also his *The Mount Vernon Papers* (New York: D. Appleton, 1860).

CHAPTER 2

1. Richard M. Upjohn, "Colonial Architecture of New York and the New England States" (president's address at 1869 AIA convention, in *Proceedings of the Third Annual Convention of the American Institute of Architects,* November 17, 1869), 549.

2. Walter Muir Whitehill, "A Centennial Sketch," in *Boston Society of Architects, the First Hundred Years, 1867–1967,* eds. Marvin E. Goody and Robert P. Walsh (Boston: Boston Society of Architects, 1967), 27.

3. M. S. [Montgomery Schuyler], "Charles Follen McKim," *Architectural Record* 26 (November 1909): 381.

4. *New York Sketch Book of Architecture* 1, no. 1 (January 1874), introductory page.

5. "Old House in Newport," *New York Sketch Book of Architecture* 1, no. 12 (December 1874), pl. 45.

6. *New York Sketch Book of Architecture* 3, no. 4 (April 1876): pl. 15; *New York Sketch Book of Architecture* 2, no. 8 (August 1875): pl. 30; *New York Sketch Book of Architecture* 3, no. 7, (July 1876): pl. 25.

7. Material from a history by Benjamin Smith in possession of family descendents. *New York Sketch Book of Architecture* 2, no. 10 (October 1875): pl. 37.

8. The term "modernized colonial" is in George William Sheldon, *Artistic Country Seats,* vol. 1 (New York: D. Appleton, 1886), 23; the term "shingle style" is from Vincent J. Scully Jr., *The Shingle Style* (New Haven: Yale University Press, 1955), and later editions.

9. Mead quoted in Moore, *The Life and Times of Charles Follen McKim,* 41.

10. Clarence Cook, "Beds and Tables, Stools and Candlesticks, VII," *Scribner's Monthly* 13 (November 1876): 90, see illus. on 88.

11. Robert S. Peabody, quoted in Wheaton A. Holden, "Robert Swain Peabody of Peabody and Stearns in Boston: The Early Years (1870–1886)" (Ph.D. diss., Boston University, 1969), 24.

12. R. S. P. [Robert S. Peabody], "A Talk about 'Queen Anne,'" *American Architect* 2 (April 28, 1877): 134.

13. Georgian [Robert S. Peabody], "Georgian Houses of New England," *American Architect* 2 (October 20, 1877): 338; this article was completed in *American Architect* 3 (February 16, 1878): 54–55. Substantially the same article had been given as a paper at the 1877 AIA convention in Boston, printed as "Colonial Architecture," in *Proceedings of the Eleventh and Twelfth Annual Conventions of the AIA* (Boston, 1879), 16–19.

14. *American Architect* 4 (February 16, 1878): 56, and plate.

15. William E. Barry, *Pen Sketches of Old Houses,* ed. Earle G. Shettleworth Jr., introduction by Kevin D. Murphy (1876; reprint, Augusta, Me.: Maine Preservation, 2002); and "Colonial Houses and Their Uses to Art," *American Architect* 3 (January 12, 1878): 12.

16. Arthur Little, *Early New England Interiors* (Boston: A. Williams, 1877). In spite of the copyright date of 1877, the book was published in 1878. Peabody's diary quoted in Holden, "Robert Swain Peabody," 81–82; Ogden Codman to Arthur Little, August 17, 1891, Codman archives, Society for the Preservation of New England Antiquities (SPNEA). See also Walter Knight Sturgis, "Arthur Little and the Colonial Revival," *Journal of the Society of Architectural Historians* 32, no. 2 (May 1973): 147–62; and Kevin Dean Murphy, "'A Stroll thro' the Past:' Three Architects of the Colonial Revival" (master's thesis, Boston University, 1985).

17. William M Woollett, *Old Homes Made New* (New York: A. J. Bicknell, 1878), 5, 7.

18. "The Need of Unity," *American Architect* 1 (January 1, 1876): 3. There had been earlier attempts at architectural journals in the United States but they quickly failed. "American Architecture-Present," *American Architect* 1 (August 5, 1876): 251. Editorial, *American Architect* 1 (September 16, 1876): 303–4; "American Architecture Past," *American Architect* 1 (July 29, 1876): 242–43. J. M. Briden, "A Few More Words about 'Queen Anne,'" *American Architect* 2 (October 6, 1877): 322.

19. "Sketches about Wethersfield, Conn., by M. P. Hapgood," *American Architect* 18 (July 18, 1885): 30; Frank E. Wallis, "Old Colonial Work, *American Architect* 19 (February 6, 1886); "Sketches at Hingham, Mass.," August 22, 1885; Glen Brown, "Old Colonial Work in Virginia and Maryland," *American Architect* 22 (October 27, November 19 and 26, 1887): 194, 198–99, 242, 254–55; A. B. Bibb, "Old Colonial Work of Virginia and Maryland," *American Architect* 24 (June 15, 1889): 279–81, is the first of seven parts that continued until vol. 34 (November 1891). William R. Ware, ed., *The Georgian Period* (Boston: American Architecture and Building News Company, 1898–1902)

20. Joseph Everett Chandler, *The Colonial Architecture of Maryland, Pennsylvania, and Virginia* (Boston: Bates, Kimball & Guild, 1892); and "Books and Papers," *American Architect* 36 (June 4, 1892): 153, 154.

21. Norman Isham and Albert F. Brown, *Early Rhode Island Houses* (Providence, Preston & Rounds, 1895); and Isham and Brown, *Early Connecticut Houses* (Providence: Preston & Rounds, 1900). James M, Lindgren, *Preserving Historic New England* (New York: Oxford University Press, 1995).

22. Montgomery Schuyler, "A History of Old Colonial Architecture," *Architectural Record* 4 (January–March 1895): 366.

23. Schuyler's career and his changing viewpoint are considered in William H. Jordy and Ralph Coe, eds., "Montgomery Schuyler," in *American Architecture and Other Writings by Montgomery Schuyler,* vol. 1 (Cambridge, Mass.: Belknap Press of Harvard University Press, 1961), 1–89; and Edward R. Smith, "Montgomery Schuyler and the History of American Architecture," *Architectural Record* 36 (September 1914): 364–66.

24. Edith Wharton and Ogden Codman, *The Decoration of Houses* (New York: Scribner's, 1897), 81–82.

25. A. C. David, "A Modern Instance of Colonial Architecture," *Architectural Record* 17 (April 1905): 305.

26. *Proceedings of the Twenty-Fourth Annual Convention . . . Washington, D. C.* (Chicago: American Institute of Architects, 1890), 33–35

27. Alice Morse Earle, *Old Time Gardens, Newly Set Forth* (New York: Macmillan, 1901); and *Sun Dials and Roses of Yesterday* (New York: Macmillan, 1902). See also her *Child Life in Colonial Days* (New York: Macmillan, 1899); *Customs and Fashions in Old New England* (New York: Scribner, 1893); *Home Life in Colonial Days* (New York: Macmillan, 1900).

On Earle see May Brawley Hill, *Grandmother's Garden: The Old-Fashioned American Garden 1865–1915* (New York: Harry N. Abrams, 1999).

28. James M. Lindgren, *Preserving the Old Dominion* (Charlottesville: University of Virginia Press, 1993).

29. See Richard Guy Wilson, "The Early Work of Charles F. McKim," *Winterthur Portfolio* 14, no. 3 (Autumn 1979): 235–67.

30. *Newport Mercury,* October 8, 1881, 1; Sheldon, *Artistic Country Seats* 1, no. 23. The rear elevation has been recently restored by the Preservation Society of Newport County; I am indebted to curator Paul Miller for this observation.

31. *Billbooks,* vol. 1, 165, 203, 358, McKim, Mead & White, The New-York Historical Society (henceforth MMW, NYHS).

32. Frank Lloyd Wright, *Genius and the Mobocracy* (1949; reprint, New York: Horizon Press, 1971), 56. Scully, *The Shingle Style;* see also Leland Roth *Shingle Styles: Innovation and Tradition in American Architecture 1874 to 1984* (New York: Harry N. Abrams, 1999).

33. Sheldon, *Artistic Country Seats,* vol. 2, 9.

34. The house was commissioned in mid-1882 but completed designs were not ready until December 1883. However, the projected cost of $67,300 for a masonry structure caused Taylor to request a frame dwelling instead. Construction began in August 1884 and was not completed until September 1886.

35. George C. Mason, "Colonial Architecture I", *American Architect* 10 (August 13, 1881): 71–74; See also *American Architect* 7 (March 20, 1880): 117.

36. McKim to Mrs. Edgar, August 21, 1895, and McKim to Tom [illegible], June 26, 1895, McKim Collection, Library of Congress, Letter book 4, nos. 292, 219.

37. Stratford Hall was illustrated in Mrs. Martha J. Lamb, *The Homes of America* (New York: Appleton, 1879), 68.

38. Sheldon, *Artistic Country Seats,* vol. 2, 25; Mariana Griswold Van Rensselaer, "American Country Dwellings," *The Century* 32 (July 1886): 428; "A Newport Dwelling," *The Art Age* 3 (December 1885): 86–87; see also *The Art Age* (January 1886): 100.

39. *Report of the Massachusetts Board of World's Fair Managers* (1894), 12, 31–32, quoted in Susan Prendergast Schoelwer, "Curious Relics and Quaint Scenes: The Colonial Revival at the Chicago's Great Fair," in Axelrod, *The Colonial Revival,* 186.

40. Quoted in *Buildings and Art and the World's Fair* (Chicago: Rand, McNally, 1894), unpaginated; see also Schoelwer, "Curious Relics and Quaint Scenes," *The Colonial Revival,* 189–90.

41. Howard Crosby Butler, "An American Style of Architecture," *The Critic* 23 (September 30, 1893): 203.

42. Catherine W. Bishir, "Landmarks of Power: Building a Southern Past," *Southern Cultures* (1993): 4–45. Thomas Nelson Page, *The Old South* (New York: Scribner's, 1893); and *In Ole Virginia* (New York: Scribner's, 1897). See also Thomas L. Connelly, *The Marble Man: Robert E. Lee and His Image in American Society* (New York: Knopf, 1977); Charles R. Wilson, *Baptized in Blood: The Religion of the Lost Cause, 1865–1920* (Athens, Ga.: n.p., 1980); and Gaines M. Foster, *Ghosts of the Confederacy: Defeat, the Lost Cause, and the Emergence of the New South, 1865–1913* (New York: Oxford University Press, 1987).

43. *Buildings and Art and the World's Fair,* unpaginated; and Kate Brannon Knight, *History of the Work of Connecticut Women at the World's Columbian Exposition* (Hartford: n.p., 1893), 15, quoted in Schoelwer, "Curious Relics and Quaint Scenes," in Axelrod, *The Colonial Revival* 191.

44. *American Architecture,* (April 6, 1895), 5. The reference is to the David Francis House by Eames and Young.

45. C. W., "Colonial Architecture for American Homes," *American Homes* (January 1897): 11–18. This magazine was published by the Knoxville, Tennessee, architect George Barber as part of his promotion for mail order plans. I am indebted to Boyd Coons for the reference.

46. "The Reminiscences of Thomas Mott Shaw," unpublished (Perry, Dean, Rogers & Partners, archives, Boston, 1956), 5.

47. Russell Claxton, "Dennis & Dennis," *Architecture/Georgia* (July 1991): 25. Much of my information on Ellis comes from the Genealogical and Historical Room at the Washington Memorial Library, Macon, Ga. I am indebted to Muriel McDowell Jackson for assistance.

48. "Types of Colonial Homes Design by Curran R. Ellis, Macon, Georgia," *Southern Architect and Building News* 21, no. 20 (December 22, 1908): 19–25 ff.

49. There is some resemblance to Asher Benjamin, *The American Builder's Companion,* 3rd ed. (Boston: R. P. & C. Williams, 1827), pl. 22; and Benjamin, *The Architect, or Complete Builder's Guide* (Boston: Benjamin B. Mussey, 1845), pl. 17.

50. "Types of Colonial Homes Design by Curran R. Ellis," *Southern Architect* 19.

51. I am greatly indebted in my research to Timothy Matthewson, former chief of interpretation and education, and to J. Nathan Campbell, curator of collections, McFaddin-Ward House, Beaumont, Texas, who shared information with me. See also Jessica Foy and Judith Linsley, *The McFaddin-Ward House* (Texas State Historical Association, 1992).

52. "Residence of W. P. H. McFaddin, Beaumont, Texas," *Southern Orchards and Homes* II (Feb. 1909), 14–15.

53. Joseph Everett Chandler, *The Colonial House* (New York: McBride, 1916), 252.

54. Mark Alan Hewitt, *The Architect and the American Country House 1890–1940* (n.p.: New Haven, 1990), 157; see also Hewitt, "Hill-Stead . . . ," *Antiques* 134 (October 1988): 849–61. Henry James, *The American Scene* (1907; reprint, New York: Horizon Press, 1967), 45–46; this originally appeared in the *North American Review* (1905). For assistance on Hill-Stead, I am indebted to Sharon Stotz, education curator, and Linda M Steigleder, director. Treatments of Hill-Stead and its design can be found in Sandra L. Katz, *Dearest of Geniuses: A Life of Theodate Pope Riddle* (Windsor, Conn.: Tide-Mark, 2003); and Sharon Dunlap Smith, *Theodate Pope Riddle, Her Life and Architecture* (n.p.: 2002). See also Barbara Donahue, *Farmington: New England Town Through Time* (Farmington, Conn.: Land Trust, 1989).

55. Theodate Pope to William R. Mead, undated (ca. June 1898), MMW, NYHS. Pope to Mead, September 17, 1898, Walker Cain Collection, Columbia University, Avery Library. Smith, *Theodate Pope Riddle,* appendix B, reproduces both letters.

56. Quoted in Smith, *Theodate Pope Riddle* chap. 4, 4; "Homelot, 'Miss Theodate Pope,' by Gordon H. Taylor, C. E., Boston, Massachusetts. September 30, 1898." The plans closest to the house as built are signed by Swarthout, February 9, 1899; a set of barn plans are signed by L. D. Ayres, November 25–30, 1898. All the drawings are in MMW, NYHS; copies in possession of Hill-Stead.

57. Pope diary, quoted in Smith, *Theodate Pope Riddle,* chap. 4, 5. Original in possession of Hill-Stead. Among the books Theodate Pope owned which showed the interior of Carter's Grove is Thomas Allen Glenn, *Some Colonial Mansions and Those Who Lived in Them* (n.p.: Philadelphia, 1899), 284. However, when she purchased the book is unknown. Most of the architecture books in the house postdate the 1901 construction. A list of the books was supplied by Sharon Stotz.

58. Theodate Pope wrote: "It must be right for father and he is 5'11" tall." Quoted in Katz, *Dearest of Geniuses,* 47.

59. James, *The American Scene,* 46. See Barr Ferree, "Notable American Homes—Hill Stead," *American Homes and Gardens* 7 (1910) 45 ff., for a description of the downstairs rooms. See also "Mr. Alfred A. Pope's House at Farmington, Conn.," *The Architectural Record* 20, no. 2 (August 1906): 122–29. Smith, *Theodate Pope Riddle,* chap. 4, 8.

60. "Traces of the Franciscans in California," *Craftsman* 1 (February 1902): 29–30. For background see Kevin Starr, *Americans and the California Dream 1850–1915* (New York: Oxford University Press, 1973); Starr, *Inventing the Dream* (New York: Oxford University Press, 1984); and Starr, *Material Dreams: Southern California Through the 1920s* (New York: Oxford University Press, 1990). See also Karen J. Weitze, *California's Mission Revival* (Los Angeles: Hennessey and Ingalls, 1984); George Wharton James, "The Influence of the 'Mission Style' upon the Civic and Domestic Architecture of Modern California," *Craftsman* 5 (February 1904): 458–69; and Arthur Burnett Benton, "Architecture for the Southwest," *Land of Sunshine* 4 (February 1896): 126–30.

61. William G. Moore, *Redlands Yesterdays* (Redlands, Calif.: Moore Historical Association, 1983).

62. "Application for Building Permit," copy in the A. K. Smiley Public Library. I am indebted for research help to Nathan D. Gonzales, asso-

ciate archivist, A. K. Smiley Public Library. "Father of Imperial Valley Tells of Valley's Rise," *Los Angeles Examiner* (January 30, 1949). See also, William F. Holt, *Memories of a Missourian* (ca. 1920; reprint, Holtville, Mo.: Tribune Printing, 1978). Although there is no supporting documentation, local legend holds that Wright wrote the novel in the Holt's stable apartment; Wright particularly acknowledges "my friend, Mr. W. F. Holt," and to him "this story is inscribed." Wright, *The Winning of Barbara Worth* (Chicago: Book Supply Co., 1911), 5.

63. Lisa Germany, *Harwell Hamilton Harris* (1991; reprint, Berkeley: University of California Press in association with the University of Texas Center for the study of American Architecture, 2000), 31–15.

64. Sarah Orne Jewett, "River Driftwood," *The Atlantic Monthly* 48 (October 1881): 500; reprinted in Jewett, *Country By-Ways* (South Berwick, Me.: Old Berwick Historical Society, 1981). Sarah Orne Jewett, *The Tory Lover* (Boston: Houghton Mifflin, 1901), 1, 7, 9, 20, 27. See also Paula Blanchard, *Sarah Orne Jewett: Her World and Her Work* (Reading, Mass.: Addison-Wesley, 1994), 314–15, and chap. 23. For the Hamilton house, I am indebted to essays and entries by Kevin D. Murphy, Richard M. Candee, Richard C. Nylander, Sandra S. Armentrout, Jessie Ravage, Philip A. Hayden, Lucinda A. Brockway, and others in Sarah L. Griffen and Kevin D. Murphy, *"A Noble and Dignified Stream": The Piscataqua Region in the Colonial Revival, 1860–1930* (York, Me.: Old York Historical Society, 1992).

65. Henry F. Withey and Elsie Rathburn Withey, *Biographical Dictionary of American Architects (Deceased)* (Los Angeles: New Age Publishing, 1956), 83, 374–75.

66. Wharton and Codman, *Decoration of Houses*, 38, 47. Edith Wharton, *Italian Villas and Their Gardens* (New York: Century, 1904), 6; the book originally appeared as articles in 1903. In addition, Charles Platt, *Italian Gardens* (New York: Harper & Brothers, 1894), certainly was influential.

67. Louise Shelton, "The Gardens at Hamilton House, South Berwick, Maine," *American Homes and Gardens* 6 (November 1909): 422–25.

68. Hildegarde Hawthorne, "A Garden of Romance: Mrs. Tyson's, at Hamilton House, South Berwick, Maine," *Century Magazine* 80 (September 1910): 778; Elsie Vaughn, "The Story of Hamilton House," typescript, ca. 1934 (SPNEA), quoted in Griffen and Murphy, *"A Noble and Dignified Stream,"* 100.

69. Ogden Codman to Arthur Little, August 17, 1891; Codman to Fiske Kimball, January 5, 1927, and March 17, 1935; Codman to William Sumner Appleton, August 12, 1931; all quoted in Pauline C. Metcalf, "Design and Decoration," and Christopher Monkhouse, "The Making of a Colonial Revival Architect," in Metcalf, ed., *Ogden Codman and the Decoration of Houses* (Boston: Godine, 1988), 5, 7, 52, 68.

70. Edith Wharton, *A Backward Glance* (New York: D. Appleton, 1934), 149; and Wharton and Codman, *The Decoration of Houses*, 81–82. See Richard Guy Wilson, "Scientific Eclecticism," in Brooklyn Museum, *The American Renaissance, 1876–1917* (Brooklyn and New York: Brooklyn Museum and Pantheon, 1979), chap. 4; and Wilson, "Edith and Ogden: Writing, Decorating and Architecture," in Metcalf, ed., *Ogden Codman*, 133–84; and Carroll L. V. Meeks, "Picturesque Eclecticism," *Art Bulletin* 32 (1950): 226–35.

71. Codman to Fiske Kimball, March 17, 1935, quoted in Metcalf, ed., *Ogden Codman*, 68. Codman to William Sumner Appleton, August 12, 1934, Codman Collection, Boston Athenaeum.

72. Metcalf, ed., *Ogden Codman*, 38, 110 ff. *New York Sketch Book of Architecture* 3 (April 1876): pl. 15. Codman to Wulff, October 15, 1910, Codman Collection, Boston Athenaeum.

73. Fiske Kimball, *Mr. Samuel McIntire, Carver, the Architect of Salem,* (Portland, Me.: The Southworth-Anthoensen Press, published for the Essex Institute of Salem, Mass., 1940).

CHAPTER 3

1. Talbot Faulkner Hamlin, *The American Spirit in Architecture* (New Haven: Yale University Press, 1926), 267. A. Lawrence Kocher, "The American Country House," *Architectural Record* 58 (November 1925): 402, 403, 405, 416. See also David Gebhard, "The Colonial Revival in the 1930s," *Winterthur Portfolio* 22, no. 2/3 (Summer/Autumn 1987): 109–48.

2. "The Story of American is the Story of Colonial Furniture," *Home Furnishing Arts* 2, no. 2 (Fall and Winter 1935): 52.

3. Russell F. Whitehead, "Status of the Country House," *Architectural Record* (November 1923): 425. " 'Nudist Homes' Giving Way to Georgian," *Richmond Times-Dispatch,* November 20, 1938, 5. Rhea Talley, "Wright Attacks 'Shallowness' of Williamsburg," *Richmond Times-Dispatch,* October 25, 1938, 1; "Segregated Architecture" *Richmond News Leader,* October 27, 1938, 3. Wright's talk was extensively covered in the Virginia press and also nationally; see: *Time,* November 7, 1939, 37; Frank Lloyd Wright, "Williamsburg," *New York Herald,* November 6, 1938, sec. 2, 8; Harold R. Shurtleff, "Reply to F. L. Wright," *Boston Transcript,* December 3, 1938, sec. 5, 5.

4. A complete bibliography would be very difficult. One attempt is Richard G. Bach, "Early American Architecture and the Allied Arts—A Bibliography," *Architectural Record* 59–60 and 63–64 (March–July 1926 and June–September 1928): 65–72, 265–73, 328–34, 483–88, 525–32, 577–80, and adv. sec. 136–40, 190–92 and adv. sec. 142, 144. See also *Colonial Revival in America: Annotated Bibliography,* n.p. On background see: William B. Rhoads, "The Discovery of America's Architectural Past, 1874–1914," and Keith N. Morgan and Richard Cheek, "History in the Service of Design," in *The Architectural Historian in America,* ed. Elisabeth Blair MacDougall, *Studies in the History of Art* 35 (Washington, D.C.: National Gallery of Art, 1990): 23–39, 61–75.

5. Newcomb, who taught at the University of Illinois, specialized in books on the colonial house and also ceramics, publishing more than twenty titles.

6. Harold Donaldson Eberlein, *The Architecture of Colonial America* (Boston: Little, Brown, 1915), v, vi.

7. "Salutation," *White Pine Series of Architectural Monographs* 1, no. 1 (July 1915). Financial arrangements changed over the course of the publication, and in 1924 the White Pine Bureau ended all advertising, but Weyerhaeuser continued to sponsor and advertise until 1932 when all support ceased. Then the series was absorbed into *Pencil Points* magazine, where it continued as a regular feature until December 1940. See Stevens R. Anderson, "Russell Whitehead and the Pencil Point Years 1925–1936: The Debate on Modern American Architecture" (master's thesis, University of Virginia, 1993). There have been several attempts to republish parts of the White Pine Series: in 1977 by the Early America Society and Arno Press, and in 1987 by the National Historical Society.

8. Aymar Embury II, "Farmhouses of New Netherlands," *White Pine Series of Architectural Monographs* 1, no. 3 (1915): 3; and Russell F. Whitehead, *Good Houses: Typical Historic Architectural Styles for Modern Wood-built Homes* (St. Paul: Weyerhaeuser Forest Products, 1922), 9.

9. Fiske Kimball, *Domestic Architecture of the American Colonies and Early Republic* (New York: Charles Scribner's Sons, 1922), xviii, 261; and Kimball, *American Architecture* (Indianapolis and New York: Bobs-Merrill, 1925), 13–14, 74.

10. Van Wyck Brooks, "On Creating a Usable Past," *Dial* 64 (April 11, 1918): 339; Lewis Mumford, *Sticks and Stones: A Study of American Architecture and Civilization* (n.p., 1924), 9–10, 30, 49, and chap. 1.

11. Nancy McClelland, *Furnishing the Colonial and Federal House* (New York: J. B. Lippincott, 1936), 7.

12. Robert and Elizabeth Shackleton, *The Quest of the Colonial* (New York: Century, 1907), 66. Robert and Elizabeth Shackleton, *The Charm of the Antique* (Philadelphia: Penn Publishing. 1914), 136, 137–38, 104–5.

13. Joseph Everett Chandler, *The Colonial House* (New York: Robert M. McBride, 1916), preface, 252, 263.

14. Philip A. Hayden, in eds. Sarah L. Griffin and Kevin Murphy *"A Noble and Dignified Stream": The Piscataqua Region in the Colonial Revival, 1860–1930* (York, Me.: Old York Historical Society, 1992), 100–104.

15. For background see Elizabeth Stillinger, *The Antiquers* (New York: Alfred A. Knopf, 1980).

16. Quoted in Samuel Chamberlain and Paul Hollister, *Beauport at Gloucester: The Most Fascinating House in America* (New York: Hastings House, 1951), 2. Beauport has been extensively published; one of the best sources is: Nancy Curtis and Richard C. Nylander, eds., *Beauport: The Sleeper-McCann House* (Boston: Society for the Preservation of New England Antiquities, 1990).

17. Reginald T. Townsend, "An Adventure in Americana: Beauport—the Residence of Henry D. Sleeper, Esq., at Gloucester, Mass. *Country Life* (February 1929), 35.

18. David Lancaster, *The History of Gilmanton* (Gilmanton, N.H.: Alfred Prescott, 1845); Jane Scriven Cumming, with Barbara Donahue, *Gilmanton Summers* (Gilmanton, N.H.: privately printed, 1993).

19. Tax records for Gilmanton are unclear as to the precise date the Watsons constructed their house. The house appears to have been built 1915–16. The building materials in the house are numbered with the Sears "Already Cut" system. Mrs. Watson in several interviews in 1971 stated they purchased their house from Sears.

20. Katherine Cole Stevenson and H. Ward Jandl, *Houses by Mail: A Guide to Houses from Sears, Roebuck and Company* (Washington, D. C.: The Preservation Press, 1986), 109, 184.

21. Quoted in Stevenson and Jandl, *Houses by Mail,* 323, 326. This is a compilation of all the catalogs. Actual copies of Sears' catalogs are scarce, they were too common to be saved. A few have been reprinted.

22. *Sears, Roebuck Catalog of Houses, 1926* (reprint of *Modern Homes, 1926*; New York: Dover, 1991), 30, 62. These models are referenced in Stevenson and Jandl, *Houses by Mail,* 325, 334.

23. Aymar Embury II, *The Dutch Colonial House: Its Origin, Design, Modern Plan, and Construction* (New York: McBride, Nast, 1913), ii, 11. See also his *One Hundred Country Houses: Modern American Examples* (New York: Century, 1909).

24. *Sears, Roebuck Catalog of Houses* (1926; reprint, New York: Dover, 1991), 57.

25. *Sears, Roebuck Home Builder's Catalog* (1910; reprint, New York: Dover, 1990), 70, 71, 87.

26. Robert Schweitzer and Michael W. R. Davis, *America's Favorite Homes: Mail-Order Catalogues as a Guide to Popular Early 20th-Century Houses* (Detroit: Wayne State University Press, 1990); David M. Schwartz, "When Home Sweet Home Was Just a Mailbox Away," *Smithsonian* 16 (November 1985): 90–99; Tim Snyder, "The Sears Pre-Cut: A Mail-Order House for Everyone," *Fine Homebuilding* 28 (February 1985–January 1986): 42–46; Shirley Maxwell and James C. Massey, "The Story on Sears," *Old House Journal* (July–August 2002): 44–51. Amanda Cooke and Avi Friedman, "Ahead of Their Time: The Sears Catalogue Prefabricated Homes," *Journal of Design History* 14, no.1 (2001): 53–70.

27. One example is Hopewell, Virginia. See Richard Guy Wilson, *Buildings of Virginia* (New York: Oxford University Press, 2002), 481.

28. Materials related to the Stevens-Coolidge Place are located at the site and also with the Trustees of Reservations archives at Castle Hill, Ipswich, Massachusetts. I am indebted to Susan Hill Dolan, historic resources manager, and Robert Murray, property manager. Information from Boston University Preservation Studies Program, "Preliminary Master Plan for the Stevens-Coolidge Place," compiled and edited by Karen Davis, 1996.

29. Helen's entry for October 22 and 31, 1915, in John Gardner Coolidge, *A War Diary in Paris 1914–1917* (Cambridge, Mass.: Riverside Press, 1931), 80, 82.

30. Quotes from Coolidge's diary in Walter Muir Whitehill, "The Stevens-Coolidge Place in North Andover," n.d., copy in Trustees files.

31. Joseph Everett Chandler, *The Colonial House* (New York: McBride, 1916), 33, 34. For background I am indebted to Thomas Denenberg, "Joseph Everett Chandler" (master's thesis, Boston University, 1995).

32. "Specifications for Alterations Top House at Andover, Mass. For Mrs. John G. Coolidge," John Everett Chandler, 1914. Also cited in Wendy Pearl, "Joseph Everett Chandler and the Stevens-Coolidge Place" (paper presented at Preservation Planning Colloquium, Boston University, December 1955), 7.

33. One example is a Hepplewhite-styled late-eighteenth-century secretary that she purchased at American Art Association, Anderson Galleries, sale no. 4232, February 8, 1936.

34. Diary entry for August 1925 quoted in "Preliminary Master Plan for the Stevens-Coolidge Place," 52.

35. Wallace Nutting, "Period Furniture," in *Wallace Nutting Checklist of Early American Reproductions* (1930; reprint, Watkins Glen, N.Y.: American Life Foundation and Study Institute, 1969). For background see Thomas Denenberg, *Wallace Nutting and the Invention of Old America* (New Haven: Yale University Press, 2003).

36. Appleton to Nutting, November 13, 1914, quoted in Denenberg, *Nutting,* 92.

37. John Albright, Orville W. Carroll, and Abbott Lowell Cummings, *Historic Structure Report: Ironmaster's House* (Denver: National Park Service, 1977).

38. Abbott Lowell Cummings, *The Frame House of Massachusetts Bay, 1625–1725* (Cambridge, Mass.: Belknap Press, 1979), 36, 144, 204–5.

39. Quoted in Denenberg, *Nutting,* 97. E. N. Hartley, *Ironworks on the Saugus* (Norman: University of Oklahoma Press, 1957).

40. Quoted in Denenberg, *Nutting,* 101; and *Hospitality Hall, The Webb-Washington-Wells House* (Framingham Center, Mass.: privately printed, ca. 1916). For information I am indebted to Donna Barron and Jennifer Eifrig of the Webb-Deane-Stevens Museum.

41. Nutting to Appleton, October 6, 1916, quoted in Denenberg, *Nutting,* 102.

42. Nutting to Appleton, March 7 1916, quoted in Denenberg, *Nutting,* 102.

43. Wallace Nutting, *Wallace Nutting's Biography* (Framingham, Mass.: Old America, 1936), 151; and information from Donna Barron.

44. Frank Lloyd Wright, "Architect, Architecture, and the Client" (1896), in *Frank Lloyd Wright Collected Writings,* ed. Bruce Brooks Pfeiffer, vol. 1 (New York: Rizzoli, 1992), 30.

45. Paul Schweikher quoted in Richard Guy Wilson, "The Styles of David Adler," in ed. Martha Thorne, *David Adler, Architect* (Chicago and New Haven: Art Institute of Chicago and Yale University Press, 2002), 27; and quoted in Richard Pratt, *David Adler* (New York: M. Evans, 1970), 15–16. See also Stephen M. Salny, *The Country Houses of David Adler* (New York: W. W. Norton, 2001).

46. Original design in the Cooper-Hewitt Museum, New York. Identification supplied by Samuel Webb, letter to the Art Institute of Chicago, July 16, 2001. See Stephen Gleissner in Thorne, ed., *David Adler,* 150–59.

47. Matlack Price, "House of William McCormick Blair, Esq., Lake Forest, Ill," *Architectural Forum* 50 (January 1929): 53, 55.

48. Augusta Owen Patterson, "On the High Bluffs of Lake Forest Near Chicago," *Town & Country* 89 (January 15, 1934): 20, 23. See also Peter Reed, in Thorne, ed., *David Adler Architect,* 198–207.

49. Salny, *Adler,* 134.

50. William Seale, *Domestic Views: Historic Properties Owned or Supported by the National Society of the Colonial Dames of America* (Washington, D.C.: AIA Press, 1992). P. Gordon B. Stillman, *One Hundred Years in New York* (New York: National Society of Colonial Dames, 1995).

51. I am indebted for information to Pauline Metcalf, "Creating 'A Dignified New Home': Richard Henry Dana Jr. and the New York Headquarters of the National Society of Colonial Dames, 1928–1930," forthcoming. See also Mary Fanton Roberts, "A House Evoking Romantic Memories," *Arts & Decoration* 35 (May 1931): 30–33, 90.

52. Richard H. Dana Jr., *Richard Henry Dana, (1879–1933) Architect* (New York: privately printed, 1965).

53. Dana to Low, September 18, 1930, cited in Metcalf, "Creating 'A Dignified New Home.'"

54. Dana to Low, June 9, 1930, cited in Metcalf, "Creating 'A Dignified New Home.'"

55. Marilyn Harper, "Recreating Virginia's Colonial Past in the Image of the Present: Three Early 20th Century Restorations" (paper delivered at the Colonial Revival Conference, Charlottesville, Virginia, 2000).

56. For background see: David Gebhard, "The Spanish Colonial Revival in Southern California (1895–1930)," *Journal of the Society of Architectural Historians* 26 (May 1967): 131–47; and Elizabeth McMillian, *California Colonial: The Spanish and Rancho Revival Styles* (Atglen, Pa.: Schiffler Publishing, 2002).

57. John Bakewell Jr., "Honor Awards of Southern California Chapter AIA" *Architect and Engineer* 89 (April 1927): 43.

58. Harris Allen, "Gentle-People's Houses," *Pacific Coast Architect* 31 (March 1927): 26. Roland Coate, "The Early California House: Blending Colonial and California Forms," *California Arts and Architecture* 35 (March 1929): 20–30. See also Lauren Weiss Bricker and Roland E. Coate, "Furthering an Architectural Inheritance," in Johnson et al., *Patterns in the California Style* (Santa Barbara: Capra Press, 1992), 43–55.

59. "Residence of Mrs. W. D. Edwards, Pasadena, California, Roland E. Coate, Architect," *Pacific Coast Architect* 31 (March 1927): 29–30. Drawings for the Edwards house are in the Coate archives at the Architectural Drawings Collection, University of California, Santa Barbara.

60. Tim Gregory, "The William D. Edwards House, A History," unpublished, copy in possession of owner.

61. Coate, "The Early California House," 20–30. See David Gebhard, "The Monterey Tradition: History Re-Ordered," *New Mexico Studies in Fine Arts* 7 (1982): 14–19; and Gebhard, "Some Additional Observations on California's Monterey Tradition," *Journal of the Society of Architectural Historians* 46 (June 1987): 157–70. The working drawings for the Lefrens house, dated between July 1 and August 28, 1933, are in the Coate archives at the Architectural Drawings Collection, University of California, Santa Barbara. My appreciation to curator Kurt Helfrich for assistance. See also "Residence of Miss Katherine Lefrens, Pasadena—Roland E. Coate, Architect," *Architectural Digest* 10, no.1 (October 1938): 100.

62. John Taylor Boyd Jr., "The Country House and the Developed Landscape," *Arts and Decoration* 31 (November 1929): 100. For background see William B. O'Neal and Christopher Weeks, *The Work of William Lawrence Bottomley in Richmond* (Charlottesville: University Press of Virginia, 1985); and Davyd Foard Hood, "William Lawrence Bottomley in Virginia" (master's thesis, University of Virginia, 1975).

63. Ellen Glasgow, *Life and Gabriella* (1916; reprint, New York: Charles Scribner's Sons, 1938), 402. See also Sarah Shields Driggs, Richard Guy Wilson, and Robert Winthrop, *Richmond's Monument Avenue* (Chapel Hill: University of North Carolina Press, 2001).

64. Ellen Glasgow, *The Woman Within* (1944; reprint, New York: Hill and Wang, 1980), 217–18.

65. William A. Lambeth and Warren H. Manning, *Thomas Jefferson as an Architect and Designer of Landscape* (Boston: Houghton Mifflin, 1913). The term *historical* is important since this excludes family memories and books published shortly after the subject's death, such as Marinina Griswold Van Rensselaer, *Richardson* (1888). For background on Jefferson's rediscovery see Richard Guy Wilson, "Jefferson's Lawn: Perceptions, Interpretations, Meanings," in Wilson, ed., *Thomas Jefferson's Academical Village: The Creation of an Architectural Masterpiece* (Charlottesville: University Press of Virginia, 1993), 47–73.

66. Kimball, *American Architecture,* 13–14, 74. For background see: Joseph Die Lehandro, "Fiske Kimball: American Renaissance Historian" (master's thesis, University of Virginia, 1982); George and Mary Roberts, *Triumph on Fairmount: Fiske Kimball and the Philadelphia Museum of Art* (Philadelphia: J. B. Lippincott, 1959); Lauren Weiss Bricker, "The Writings of Fiske Kimball," *The Architectural Historian in America* 35 (Washington, D.C.: National Gallery of Art, 1990), 215–35. In addition to some of Kimball's papers, which are at the University of Virginia Special Collections, and include plans for Shack Mountain, I am indebted to Calder Loth's analysis of the house.

67. Interview with Claudine Lindberg, November 21, 2002. Georgian [Robert S. Peabody], "Georgian Houses of New England," *American Architect and Building News* 2 (October 20, 1877): 338–39; and *American Architect and Building News* 10 (November 26, 1881).

68. Elizabeth Dowling, *American Classicist: The Architecture of Philip Trammel Shutze* (New York: Rizzoli, 1989), 88.

69. Louis Bromfield, "The Midwest," in *Look at America: The Midwest,* editors of *Look* in collaboration with Louis Bromfield (Boston: Houghton Mifflin with Cowles Magazines, 1947), 21; and I. T. Frary, *Early Homes of Ohio* (Richmond, Va.: Garrett & Massie, 1936).

70. *Vanity Fair,* 1928, quoted in Carolyn V. Platt, "Bromfield's Farm," *Timeline* 13, no. 3 (May–June 1996): 40; and Louis Bromfield, *The Farm* (Cleveland: World Publishing, 1945), 342. I am indebted to Platt and also Barbara Powers, "Louis Bromfield's Malabar Farm, Form Follows Fiction," forthcoming; and David D. Anderson, *Louis Bromfield* (New York: Twayne Publishers, 1964).

71. Quoted in *Mansfield New Journal,* n.d., in Malabar Farm State Park clipping files, cited in Powers.

72. Selections from these books are collected in *Louis Bromfield at Malabar,* ed. Charles E. Little (Baltimore: Johns Hopkins University Press, 1988).

73. Louis Bromfield, *Pleasant Valley* (New York: Harper and Brothers,

1945), 70, 72, 73; and Louis Andre Lamoreux, "An Architect's Story of Louis Bromfield's Big House at Malabar," *Cleveland Plain Dealer,* March 3, 1957, 5–7, 24–27, and March 10, 1957, 34–36.

74. Frary, *Early Homes of Ohio,* pl. 110, 111, 112, and pp. 167–69. Bromfield, *Pleasant Valley,* 77–78.

75. Bromfield, *Pleasant Valley,* 79.

76. Jane Ware, *Building Ohio: A Traveler's Guide to Ohio's Rural Architecture* (Wilmington, Oh.: Orange Frazer Press, 2002), 89.

77. John D. Rockefeller Jr., "The Genesis of the Williamsburg Restoration," *National Geographic* 71 (April 1937): 401.

78. W. A. R. Goodwin, "The Restoration of Colonial Williamsburg," *National Geographic* 71 (April 1937): 410, 426–27, 441. The materials on Williamsburg are overwhelming. In addition to those cited elsewhere, the most important are: Edward A. Chappell, "Architects of Colonial Williamsburg," in *Encyclopedia of Southern Culture,* eds. C. R. Wilson and W. Ferris (Chapel Hill: University of North Carolina Press, 1989), 59–61; Thomas H. Taylor Jr., "The Williamsburg Restoration and Its Reception by the American Public, 1926–1942 (Ph.D. diss., George Washington University, 1989); George Yetter, *Williamsburg Before and After* (Williamsburg: Colonial Williamsburg Foundation, 1988); Charles B. Hosmer, *Preservation Comes of Age* (Charlottesville: University Press of Virginia, 1981), chap.1.

79. Michale Olmert, "The New, No-Frills Williamsburg," *Historic Preservation* 37 (October 1985): 27–33; and Charles B. Hosmer, "The Colonial Revival in the Public Eye: Williamsburg and the Early Garden Restoration," in ed. Alan Axelrod, *The Colonial Revival in America* (New York: W. W. Norton, 1985).

80. Hiram J. Herbert, "Williamsburg: The Ideal Home Town," *Better Homes and Gardens* 14 (July 1936): 15.

81. "Restoration of Colonial Williamsburg," *Architectural Record* 78 (December 1935), entire issue.

82. "What Williamsburg Means to Architecture," *House and Garden* 72 (November 1937): 42, 45. The entire issue was devoted to Colonial Williamsburg. The magazine published three house designs (pages 69–80) by Perry, Shaw & Hepburn based on Williamsburg models.

83. William Olivers Stevens, *Old Williamsburg and Her Neighbors* (New York: Dodd, Mead, 1938), 332–33.

84. Hiram J. Herbert, "Williamsburg: The Ideal Home Town," *Better Homes and Gardens* 14, no. 7 (July 1936): 75.

85. Richardson Wright, "Williamsburg," *House and Garden* 72, no. 5 (November 1937): 41.

86. Robert A. M. Stern, *Pride of Place: Building the American Dream* (Boston: Houghton Mifflin, 1986), 331–32.

87. Jura Koncius, "Hear Ye! Hear Ye! Colonial Williamsburg," *Washington Post,* November 30, 2003, F1, 5, 14.

CHAPTER 4

1. Henry-Russell Hitchcock, *Rhode Island Architecture* (Providence: Rhode Island Museum Press, 1939), 60; Hitchcock, introduction to *Built in USA: Post-War Architecture,* eds. Hitchcock and Arthur Drexler (New York: Museum of Modern Art, 1952), 11. Hitchcock, *The Architecture of H. H. Richardson and His Times* (New York: Museum of Modern Art, 1936). See Hitchcock's later revised view: *Richardson as a Victorian Architect* (Baltimore: Smith College and Barton-Gillet, 1966).

2. Among many writings the most significant are: Sigfried Giedion, *Space, Time, and Architecture: The Growth of a New Tradition* (Cambridge, Mass.: Harvard University Press, 1941); and Nikolaus Pevsner, *Pioneers of Modern Design from William Morris to Walter Gropius* (New York: Museum of Modern Art, 1936).

3. Examples are: Hugh Morrison, *Early American Architecture* (New York: Oxford University Press, 1952); William H. Pierson Jr., *American Buildings and Their Architects,* vol. 1, *The Colonial and Neoclassical Styles* (Garden City, N.Y.: Doubleday, 1970); and Marcus Whiffen, *The Eighteenth-Century Houses of Williamsburg: A Study of Architecture and Building in the Colonial Capital of Virginia* (Williamsburg: Colonial Williamsburg Foundation, 1960).

4. Vincent Scully, *The Shingle Style* (New Haven: Yale University Press, 1955), 151.

5. Kenneth L. Ames, introduction to *The Colonial Revival in America,* ed. Alan Axelrod (New York: Norton, 1985), 14.

6. Vincent Scully, "Back to the Future, With a Detour through Miami," *New York Times,* January 27, 1991, sec. 2, 32. Scully, "Seaside and New Haven," in Andres Duany and Elizabeth Plater-Zyberk, *Towns and Town Making Principles* (Cambridge, Mass., and New York: Harvard Graduate School of Design and Rizzoli, 1991), 17–20. See also Scully, *Modern Architecture and Other Essays,* selected by Neil Levine (Princeton: Princeton University Press, 2003).

7. Home Planners Incorporated in Farmington Hills, Michigan, published books such as *The Essential Guide to Early American Home Plans* (1987).

8. The Secretary of the Interior's Standards for the Treatment of Historic Properties, 1995.

9. Robert Venturi, *Complexity and Contradiction in Architecture* (New York: Museum of Modern Art, 1966); Brent Brolin, *The Failure of Modern Architecture* (New York: Van Nostrand Reinhold, 1976); Jane Jacobs, *The Death and Life of Great American Cities* (New York: Vintage Books, 1961); and Peter Blake, *Form Follows Fiasco: Why Modern Architecture Hasn't Worked* (Boston: Little, Brown, 1977).

10. William R. Mitchell Jr., *Edward Vason Jones* (Savannah: Martin-St. Martin, 1995). Rod Andrew Miller, "Jens Fred Larsen and American Collegiate Georgian Architecture" (Ph.D. diss., University of Louisville, 1998).

11. Jay E. Cantor, *Winterthur,* revised edition (New York: Harry N. Abrams, 1997).

12. "Royal Barry Wills," *Life* 21, no. 9 (August 26, 1946): 67–72; "Eight Houses for Modern Living," *Life* 5, no. 13 (September 26, 1938): 44–67; and *Architectural Forum* 69, no. 5 (November 1938): 312–48. The books by Wills, all of which had multiple editions, are: *Houses for Good Living* (New York: Architectural Book Publishing, 1940); *Better House for Budgeters* (New York: Architectural Book Publishing, 1941); and *Houses for Homemakers* (New York: Watts, 1945).

13. Arnold Nicholson, "Big Man in Small Houses," *Saturday Evening Post* 230, no. 39 (March 29, 1958): 36.

14. Royal Barry Wills, "Confessions of a Cape Codder," *Architectural Record* 105, no. 4 (April 1949): 132–34. David Gebhard, "Royal Barry Wills," *Winterthur Portfolio* 27, no. 1 (Spring 1992): 45–74, is the best treatment of the Wills. See also "The New England Tradition and Royal Barry Wills," *House and Home* 17, no.2 (February 1960): 97–109.

15. Royal Barry Wills Associates, *Houses for Good Living* (New York: Architectural Book Publishing, 1993), 74.

16. Information supplied by Richard Wills.

17. William R. Mitchell Jr., *The Architecture of James Means, Georgia Classicist* (Atlanta: Southern Architecture Foundation, 2001); see also Mrs. J. Ray Efird, ed., *The Houses of James Means* (Atlanta: n.p., 1979); Van Jones Martin and William Robert Mitchell, *Landmarks Homes of Georgia, 1733–1983* (Savannah: Golden Coast, 1982), 218–23.

18. Interview with Mrs. Thomas (Peggy Sheffield) Martin, April 3 and November 29, 2002. Spencer Tunnell assisted with research.

19. Interview with Mrs. Martin.

20. For much of my information, I am indebted to David H. Sachs, *The Life and Work of the Twentieth-Century Louisiana Architect A. Hays Town* (Lewiston, N.Y.: Edwin Mellen Press, 2003). See also Cyrill Vetter and Philip Gould, *The Louisiana Houses of A. Hays Town* (Baton Rouge: Louisiana State University Press, 1999); A. Hays Town, *The Architectural Style of A. Hays Town* (Baton Rouge: Amdulane Publications, 1985).

21. Lewis Mumford, "Skyline," *New Yorker* (April 30, 1938): 50. In addition to appearing in several editions of *Architectural Concrete* in 1938, the firm's work appeared in *Architectural Forum* 68 (February 1938): 137–43; and "Design Decade," *Architectural Forum* 73 (October 1940): 301; *L'Architecture D'aujourd Hui* (August 1938): 58; *Pencil Points* (April 1939): 216; *Architectural Record* 84 (August 1938): 111; and others.

22. Robert A. Ivy Jr., "Master of Creole Architecture," *Southern Accents* 17 (September/October 1994): 186–93; Linda Hallam, "By the Master of Louisiana Style," *Southern Living* 23 (September 1988): 148–50.

23. Sachs, *Town,* 88. Linda Hallam, "The Art and Architecture of a Louisiana Legend," *Southern Living* 25 (October 1990): 82.

24. Hallam, "The Art and Architecture of a Louisiana Legend," 84.

25. Information supplied by Hugh Newell Jacobsen. "Palladion Auf Amerikanisch [Palladio, American Style]," *Hauser* (June 1991): 132–39; Robert Campbell, "Palladian Abstractions," *Architectural Digest* (December 1990): 144–51.

26. *Hugh Newell Jacobsen, Architect: Recent Work* (Rockport, Mass., and Washington, D.C.: Rockport Publishers and the American Institute of Architects Press, 1994), 172–79.

27. Allan Greenberg, "What is Modern Architecture? An American Perspective," in *Allan Greenberg, Selected Works* (London: Academy Editions, 1995), 11, 13.

28. Allan Greenberg, *George Washington Architect* (New York and London: Andreas Papadakis Publisher, 1999), 90. See also Allan Greenberg, "Architecture," in ed. Wendell Garrett, *George Washington's Mount Vernon* (New York: Monacelli Press, 1998), 46–63.

29. Robert Venturi and Denise Scott Brown, *A View from the Campidoglio* (New York: Harper & Row, 1984), 100–103.

30. "The Ionic Man," *Departures* (May–June 1999). Information on the project is derived from conversations and communications with Allan Greenberg.

31. Robert A. M. Stern, *Pride of Place: Building the American Dream* (Boston: Houghton Mifflin, 1986), 3, 9, 331–32.

32. Robert A. M. Stern, *Robert A. M. Stern Buildings and Projects,* ed. Luis F. Rueda (New York: Rizzoli, 1986), 6–7.

33. Stern to author, December 10, 2003, and Stern quoted in Philip Nobel, "A Shining Lone Star," *Architectural Design* 60 (October 2003): 270–76, 281.

34. Woodside Hall, Cooperstown, 1829, is illustrated in *Historic American Buildings,* vol. 5 (New York: Garland Publishing, 1979), 197; see also the Williams-Childs house, in nearby Oaksville, Otsego County, 198.

35. Patricia Leigh Brown, "Architecture's Young Old Fogies," *New York Times,* February 9, 1995, sec. C, 1, 6. Information supplied by Fairfax and Sammons; see also *A Decade of Art and Architecture 1992–2002,* (New York: Institute of Classical Architecture, 2003), 55–58.

36. Richard Sammons to author, October 22 and 28, 2003.

37. Richard Sammons to author, October 28, 2003.

38. Charles Caleb Colton, *Lacon; or, Many Things in Few Words, Addressed to Those Who Think* (London: n.p., ca. 1820).

39. Umberto Eco, *Travels in Hyperreality* (1975; reprint, Orlando: Harcourt Brace Jovanovich, 1986), 3–58.

Acknowledgments

I owe a great debt of gratitude to many individuals and organizations who over the years have assisted my research, opened their doors, and made suggestions.

This book is dependent on the scholarship of a number of individuals:
Lauren Weiss Bricker
Joseph T. Butler
Thomas Denenberg
Leonard K. Eaton
Shaun Eyring
The late David Gebhard
Pat P. Gebhard
Mark Hewitt
Calder Loth
James Massey
Pauline Metcalf
Barbara Mitnick
Kevin Murphy
Dianne Pilgrim
William B. Rhodes
David H. Sachs
Judith Tankard
Kristina Wilson

I also owe a thank you to the many students I have been lucky to teach over the years and to whose research and scholarship I am indebted. Among them special notice to:
Stevens Anderson
Sara Sally Butler
Boyd Coons
Margaret Gruibak
Dale Gyure
Joseph Dye Lehandro
Donald Matteson
Laurie Ossman
Barbara Powers
Annie Robinson
Spencer Tunnell
Marc Wagner

Also at the University of Virginia, I owe a debt of gratitude to the library staff who have assisted over the years including Jennifer Parker and Ann Burns. Among many museums, historic houses, architect offices, libraries, and individuals, I would like to acknowledge:
Brick Store Museum, Kennebunk, Maine
National Park Service, Vassall-Craigie-Longfellow House, Cambridge, Massachusetts, Janice Hodson, Supervisory Museum Curator
Sunnyside, Tarrytown, New York
Malabar Farm, Mansfield, Ohio
Colonial Williamsburg, Ed Chappel and Carl Lounsbury
Allan Greenberg, FAIA
Hill-Stead, Linda Steigleder, Cindy Cormier, and Sharon Stotz
Hugh Newell Jacobsen, FAIA
McFaddin-Ward House, Timothy Matthewson and J. Nathan Campbell
National Society of Colonial Dames in the State of New York, Margaret Warner
Society for the Preservation of New England Antiquities, Diane Viera, president; Susanna Crampton, director of public relations; and Lorna Condon, archivist
Preservation Society of Newport County, Paul Miller
A. K. Smiley Public Library, Nathan D. Gonzales
Robert A. M. Stern and Peter Morris Dixon of Robert A. M. Stern Architects
Webb-Deane-Stevens Museum, Wethersfield, Connecticut, Donna Baron, curator, and Jennifer S. Eifrig, director
Saugus Ironworks National Historic Site, Carl Salmons-Perez, curator
Town Construction, Mr. A. Hays Town Jr.
Trustees of Reservations, Susan Hill Dolan and Robert Murray
University of California, Santa Barbara, Architectural Drawings Collection, Kurt Helfrich
Washington Memorial Library, Macon, Georgia , Muriel M. Jackson
Richard Wills, AIA, of Royal Barry Wills Associates
Anne Fairfax and Richard Sammons
1842 Inn, Macon, Georgia, Nozario Filipponi
Gilbert and Susan Bennett
Mr. and Mrs. Stewart Greene
Mr. and Mrs. John Bryan Jr.
Brad and Dorothee Cole
Mrs. John C. Cushman
Mr. Ronald Fleming
Dr. & Mrs. Charles Greeson
Eric and Claudine Lindberg
Mrs. Thomas Martin
Mrs. Bedford Moore
Mr. and Mrs. Raymond Orf
Mrs. Wesley Ru
Jack & Mary Spain
Mr. Herbert Stride
Mr. Doug Towle

Finally, I should note Ellie, who has spent too many years looking at various buildings with me, and also Kristina, David, and Abby, who have tagged along on different voyages of discovery.

Index

To Ellie

———

EDITOR: Ron Broadhurst
COPY EDITOR: Sigi Nacson
DESIGNER: Laura Lindgren
PRODUCTION MANAGER: Justine Keefe
EDITORIAL CONCEPT DEVELOPMENT: Richard Olsen

FRONT COVER: Henry Conrad Mauer, McFaddin-Ward House, Beaumont, Texas, 1906.
BACK COVER: Anne Fairfax and Richard Sammons, Farmlands, Cooperstown, New York, 2002. Entrance hall.
PAGE 1: Herbert W. C. Browne, Hamilton House, South Berwick, Maine, 1787, with additions 1899 onward. Detail of wall painting in parlor.
PAGES 2 AND 3: Henry Davis Sleeper, Beauport, Gloucester, Massachusetts, 1907–34. Library.

Published in 2004 by Harry N. Abrams, Incorporated, New York

Library of Congress Cataloging-in-Publication Data

Wilson, Richard Guy, 1940–
    The colonial revival house / by Richard Guy Wilson ; photography by Noah Sheldon.
        p.   cm.
    Includes bibliographical references and index.
    ISBN 0-8109-4959-8 (hardcover)
    1. Colonial revival (Architecture)—United States. 2. Domestic architecture—United States. 3. Architecture—United States—19th century. 4. Architecture—United States—20th century. I. Sheldon, Noah. II. Title.

NA7207.W57 2004
728'.37'0973—dc22   2004003146

Plan illustrations by John McKenna

Printed and bound in China
10 9 8 7 6 5 4 3 2 1

Harry N. Abrams, Inc.
100 Fifth Avenue
New York, N.Y. 10011
www.abramsbooks.com

Abrams is a subsidiary of

LA MARTINIÈRE
GROUPE